The Village Against the World

The Village Against the World

by
DAN HANCOX

VERSO

London • New York

First published by Verso 2013
Text © Dan Hancox
Photographs © Dave Stelfox 2013

1 3 5 7 9 10 8 6 4 2

Verso
UK: 6 Meard Street, London W1F 0EG
US: 20 Jay Street, Suite 1010, Brooklyn, NY 11201
www.versobooks.com

Verso is the imprint of New Left Books

ISBN-13: 978-1-78168-130-5

British Library Cataloguing in Publication Data
A catalogue record for this book is available from the British Library.

Library of Congress Cataloging-in-Publication Data
A catalog record for this book is available from the Library of Congress.

Typeset in Fournier by Hewer Text UK Ltd, Edinburgh, Scotland
Printed in the US by Maple Press

To Javi. Seriously, let me get the next round.

No one can stop us. There is not enough blood, nor enough walls, to prevent that one day, land, rights, and, of course, liberty will be achieved by everyone.

Marinaleda: Andaluces, levantaos,
Juan Manuel Sánchez Gordillo, 1980

Contents

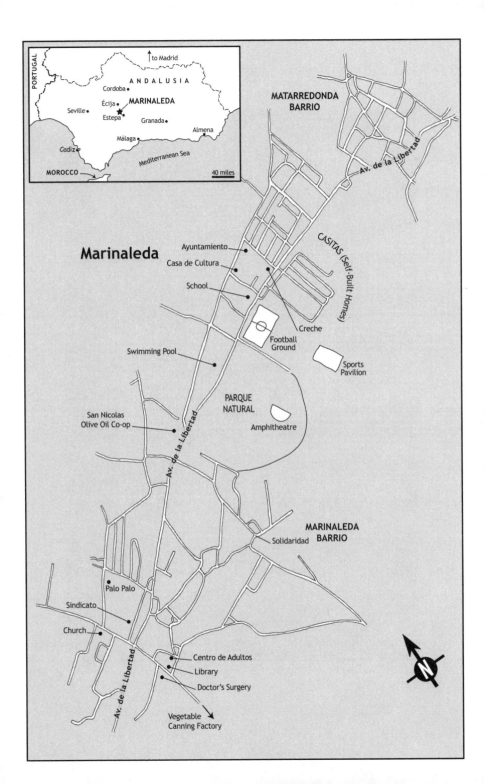

Marinaleda

to Madrid

PORTUGAL

ANDALUSIA

Cordoba
Écija
MARINALEDA
Seville
Estepa
Granada
Almena
Málaga
Cadiz
Mediterranean Sea
MOROCCO

40 miles

MATARREDONDA
BARRIO

Av. de la Libertad

CASITAS (Self-Built Homes)

Ayuntamiento

Casa de Cultura

School

Creche

Football
Ground

Sports
Pavilion

Swimming Pool

PARQUE
NATURAL

San Nicolas
Olive Oil Co-op

Amphitheatre

Av. de la Libertad

MARINALEDA
BARRIO

Solidaridad

Palo Palo

Sindicato

Church

Centro de Adultos

Library

Doctor's Surgery

Vegetable
Canning Factory

Av. de la Libertad

N

1

Meet the Village

For as long as human beings have dreamed, they have dreamed of creating a better world. The year 2016 will mark the 500th anniversary of Thomas More's *Utopia*, his short book describing the fictional island of Utopia, a regimented but model community, whose name in Greek means 'no place'. In the contemporary imagination, utopia has usually meant exactly this – no place real at any rate; nowhere actually existing. A utopia is a projection of our disappointment with the real world around us, a photo-negative of its manifold injustices, and our weaknesses as a species. We are always disappointed, so we dream of better.

We are used to the idea of utopia as an imagined place. It's often a community located in an alternative, fictional reality; on earth, or in another universe. A made-up world, where the plot twist is often that although this place seems like paradise, it is really built on lies and horror. The stories we tell ourselves are full of cautionary tales that not only is building paradise an impossibility – even attempting to build it is dangerous and hubristic. Aim high, and you will fall further.

If it's not a projection into a made-up world, utopia is an idealised vision of the future, a manifestation of a political or religious project, a blueprint for how we should all live our lives – and one day, if you would only join the party, or the church, perhaps we all will. These, like the literary utopias, are usually abstract intellectual exercises, rather than concrete attempts to forge a new community. But what if you actually tried to build utopia? How do you go from a fevered dream, an aspirational blueprint, to concrete reality?

In 2004, I was leafing through a travel guide to Andalusia while on holiday in Seville, and read a fleeting reference to a small, remote village called Marinaleda – a unique place, 'a communist utopia' of revolutionary farm labourers, it said. I was immediately fascinated, but I could find almost no details to feed my fascination. There was so little information about the village available beyond that short summary, either in the guidebook, on the internet, or on the lips of strangers I met in Seville. 'Ah yes, the strange little communist village, the utopia', a few of them said. But none of them had visited, or knew anyone who had – and no one could tell me whether it really was a utopia. The best anyone could do was to add the information that it had a charismatic, eccentric mayor, with a prophet's beard and an almost demagogic presence, called Juan Manuel Sánchez Gordillo.

Eventually I found out more. The first part of Marinaleda's miracle is that when their struggle to create utopia began, in the late 1970s, it was from a position of abject poverty. The village was suffering over 60 per cent unemployment; it was a farming community with no land, its people frequently forced to go without food for days at a time, in a period of Spanish history mired in uncertainty after the death of the fascist dictator General Franco. The second part of Marinaleda's miracle is that over three extraordinary decades, they won. Some distance along that remarkable journey of struggle and sacrifice, in 1985, Sánchez Gordillo told the newspaper *El País*:

> We have learned that it is not enough to define utopia, nor is it enough to fight against the reactionary forces. One must build it here and now, brick by brick, patiently but steadily, until we can make the old dreams a reality: that there will be bread for all, freedom among citizens, and culture; and to be able to read with respect the word 'peace'. We sincerely believe that there is no future that is not built in the present.

As befits a rebel icon, Sánchez Gordillo is fond of quoting Che Guevara; specifically Che's maxim that 'only those who dream will someday see their dreams converted to reality'. As I was to discover, in one small village in southern Spain, this isn't just a t-shirt slogan.

The heart of Andalusia is a wild place. For many years, the centre of this great region was 'the cradle of banditry', where the infamous *bandoleros* roamed. They were the celebrities of their day, the people's heroes who robbed from the rich and gave, occasionally, to the poor. Centred around the Sierra Sur mountains, it is an area historically populated by vast tracts of farmland, impoverished landless labourers and popular outlaws – and arrayed against them, the aristocratic landlords, the bourgeois political class, and the hired goons of the powerful: the detested military police force, the Guardia Civil. Spain, wrote Albert Camus, is 'the native land of the rebel, where the greatest masterpieces are cries uttered towards the impossible', and those cries resound loudest of all in Andalusia.

Andalusia is the second largest of Spain's seventeen autonomous communities, and a region which is much more than a region – it's a sin of omission to call it 'the southern bit of Spain'. Andalusia has a unique culture and politics, and, more than anything, a unique personality. Its history is marked by a succession of class wars and civil wars, invasions, conquests, uprisings, mutinies and riots, where in spite of these sporadic, often violent disruptions, the quiet but unadorned rhythms of peasant life have remained largely unchanged for millennia. The latest disturbance brought down upon the heads of the Andalusian people is, like the Inquisition, the *Reconquista* and the Spanish Civil War before it, one they had no responsibility for.

In spring 2013 unemployment in Andalusia is a staggering 36 per cent; for those aged sixteen to twenty-four, the figure is above 55 per cent – figures worse even than the egregious national average. The construction industry boom of the 2000s saw the coast cluttered with cranes and encouraged a generation to skip the end of school and take the €40,000-a-year jobs on offer on the building sites. That work is gone, and nothing is going to replace it. With the European Central Bank looming ominously over his shoulder, Prime Minister Mariano Rajoy has introduced labour reforms to make it much easier for businesses to sack their employees, quickly and with less compensation, and these new laws are now cutting swathes through the Spanish workforce in private and public sectors alike.

Spain experienced a massive housing boom from 1996 to 2008. The price of property per square metre tripled in those twelve years: its scale is now tragically reflected in its crisis. Nationally, up to 400,000 families have been evicted since 2008. Again, it is especially acute in the south: forty families a day in Andalusia have been turfed out of their homes by the banks. To make matters worse, under Spanish housing law, when you're evicted by your mortgage lender, that isn't the end of it: you have to keep paying the mortgage. In final acts of helplessness, suicides by homeowners on the brink of foreclosure have become horrifyingly common – on more than one occasion, while the bailiffs have been coming up the stairs, evictees have hurled themselves out of upstairs windows.

When people refer to *la crisis* in Spain they mean the Eurozone crisis, an economic crisis; but the term means more than that. It is a systemic crisis, a political ecology crack'd from side to side: a crisis of seemingly endemic corruption across the country's elites, including politicians, bankers, royals and bureaucrats, and a crisis of faith in the democratic settlement established after the death of Franco in 1975. A poll conducted by the (state-run) Spanish Centre for Sociological Research, in December 2012, found that 67.5 per cent of Spaniards said they were unhappy with the way their democracy works. It's this disdain for the Spanish state in general, rather than merely the effects of the economic crisis, that brought eight million *indignados* onto the streets in the spring and summer of 2011, and informed their rallying cry *¡Democracia Real YA!*: real democracy now.

Even before the crisis descended on Spain, the wealth gap in Andalusia was a chasm. It has been so forever. It is a region where mass rural pauperism exists alongside vast aristocratic estates – the *latifundios*, the South-American-style mega-estates owned by the Spanish nobility. It's an often-repeated bit of southern rural mythology that you can walk all the way from Seville, the Andalusian capital, to the northern coast of Spain without ever leaving the land of the notorious Duchess of Alba, a woman thought to have more titles than anyone else in the world. While 22.5 per cent of

her fellow Spaniards are forced to survive on only €500 a
month, the *duquesa* is estimated to be worth €3.2 billion –
and still receives €3 million a year in EU farm subsidies.

In one small village in Andalusia's wild heart, there lies
stability and order. Like Asterix's village impossibly holding out against the Romans, in this tiny *pueblo* a great
empire has met its match, in a ragtag army of boisterous
upstarts yearning for liberty. The bout seems almost laugh-
ably unfair – Marinaleda's population is 2,700, Spain's is 47
million – and yet the empire has lost, time and time again.

Sixty miles east of the regional capital, Seville, ninety
miles from Granada and its Alhambra, sixty-five miles
inland from Malaga and the Costa del Sol, surrounded by
endless expanses of farmland, sits Marinaleda. The nearest 'big town', with supermarkets and roundabouts and
other such urban affectations, is Estepa, six miles away –
and even its population is only 12,000. Marinaleda's bus
stop sees two buses a day, one going to Seville and one
coming the other way, and there is no train route for
miles around. But then Marinaleda is not really on the
way to anywhere.

Nothing is known of any possible Roman, Carthaginian
or Moorish forebears, although these peoples left quite a
mark on the rest of the region. The first record of the
village's existence is in the early 1600s, as part of the
Marquis of Estepa's farmlands, when landless labourers
toiling over the wheat and olive crops set up there to be

closer to their work, and to the water from the nearby Salado Creek.

Driving through the south, it can be hard to spot the signs of the crisis that is ravaging it. The olive plantations cover Andalusia in a sprawling camouflage, like those big nets army cadets have to crawl under, roughly stitched together and spread out like a blanket over the gentle undulations of the landscape. Occasional wheat fields and almond or orange trees interrupt the olive rows, along with some empty fields, lying fallow for four years or more while the soil replenishes itself. Sometimes a farmhouse nestles amid this pattern, many of which are ruins from another era, ceilings gone, half-crumbled walls adorned with chipped whitewash and graffiti.

Although Marinaleda is in a part of Andalusia known as the Sierra Sur, the southern highlands, here on the broad plain of the Genil River there is only one range of any significant elevation for miles around. High up one of these hills sits Estepa; if you climb up just a little from the town centre, you can see across whole regions. On my first visit to Estepa, I met a young woman from Oregon called Robyn, who was doing a year's English teaching in Andalusia. With some Spanish friends we went for a walk up to the top, to look down on the fields and see if we could spot Marinaleda.

The air up there was packed with invisible dust. It tingled on the tongue and constantly assailed the skin – the dust in this part of the world is impossible to ignore, especially if you're not used to it. Robyn was more than familiar with it, but had just returned from a short holiday in the UK, and the sudden change from the all-pervasive London damp to Andalusia's bone-dry winter air chapped her lips to the point that they were actually bleeding. She dabbed the blood away, but it just kept coming.

You have to go further south than the Sierra Sur before you encounter clear reminders that this land was once the Al-Andalus of the Moorish Caliphs. South, towards Granada and the coast, where some of the road signs are written in English and Arabic as well as Spanish, and there are advertisements for ferry tickets from Algeciras for Morocco, and North African restaurants and coffee houses. Even when Andalusia's extraordinary history is concealed from view, a great deal has endured for centuries – in the day-to-day life and spirit of the people, and the attachment to the land.

Looking south across Marinaleda from my landlord Antonio's whitewashed balcony, which is a heat trap even when the temperature peaks at sixteen degrees Celsius, as it normally does in winter, the only visible difference from a century ago are the spiky TV aerials, the spindly church weathervanes of this predominantly secular community. Otherwise, the residential part of the village appears the same as it ever was. The leaves on the orange trees stir reluctantly in the intermittent breeze, a chicken wanders past a man in blue overalls turning over the soil in his vegetable garden.

Little of the farming is actually done directly next to the village. El Humoso, the 1,200-hectare farm owned by the village co-operative, is several miles away. However, there is one olive oil processing plant in the village itself, providing a heavenly scent to counterbalance the exhaust fumes from the main road. And on the fringes of the village there are numerous big sheds and garages with dark, open interiors and clumsy, lethal-looking farm equipment. Tractors and trailers and things with big metal teeth and spikes – and occasionally sparks from the soldering iron. Then there is the sizeable vegetable processing and canning factory on the edge of the village, built to create more work for the co-operative in the 1990s, proudly adorned with massive paintings of pimentos and artichokes.

If you stand in the right spot near La Bodega, the restaurant on the very edge of the village, the factory building blocks out Estepa, to the south, and you really could be in the only village in the world. The hills behind Estepa, once swarming with bandits, are the only bumps in the skyline you can see from Marinaleda, and even those are usually obscured when you're in the midst of the village. If you head further out, towards and beyond Marinaleda's cemetery, with its twelve-foot walls and centuries of resting Carmens and Antonios, and walk through the fields to the north, on the dirt tracks across slender, underwatered streams, you can see Estepa much better: the parent town sitting prettily on the balcony surveying the region, the basin below.

It may be a household name in Spain today, but it was not until the late twentieth century that Marinaleda gained any notoriety. The village's first victories came during a different systemic crisis, one which exists in the living memory of many: the aftermath of a fascist dictatorship. In 1975, thirty-six years after his brutal victory in the Spanish Civil War, General Francisco Franco finally passed away. He left Andalusia in a wretched state: aside from the embryonic construction and tourism industries on the Costa del Sol – the profits from which rarely enriched the locals – the region was bereft of industrial development, and of investment generally. As a region historically home to rebellious peasant farmers, scourges of the kind of central authority Franco embodied, and his enemies in the 1936–39 Civil War, he had been happy to let it rot.

In the ensuing chaos of the dictator's death, while his friends and enemies manoeuvred to address the power vacuum in Madrid, the small community of poor, mostly landless farm labourers in Marinaleda began to pursue their own unique version of *la Transición*. At the time, 90 per cent of landless day labourers, known in Spain as *jornaleros*, had to feed themselves and their families on only two months of work a year.

As Spain began its slow, careful transition from fascism to liberal democracy, the people of Marinaleda formed a political party and a trade union, and began fighting for land and freedom. There followed over a decade of unceasing struggle, in which they occupied airports, train stations, government buildings, farms and palaces; went on hunger strike, blocked roads, marched, picketed, went on hunger strike again; were beaten, arrested and tried countless times for their pains. Astonishingly, in 1991 they prevailed. The government, exhausted by their defiance, gave them 1,200 hectares of land belonging to the Duke of Infantado, head of one of Spain's oldest and wealthiest aristocratic families.

From the very beginning, one man was at the forefront of this struggle. In 1979, at the age of thirty, Juan Manuel Sánchez Gordillo became the first elected mayor of Marinaleda, a position he has held ever since – re-elected time after time with an overwhelming majority. However, holding official state-sanctioned positions of power was only a distraction from the serious business of *la lucha* – the struggle. In the intense heat of the summer of 1980, the village launched 'a hunger strike against hunger' which brought them national and even global recognition. Everything they have done since that summer has increased the notoriety of Sánchez Gordillo and his village, and added to their admirers and enemies across Spain.

Sánchez Gordillo's philosophy, outlined in his 1980 book *Andaluces, levantaos*, and in countless speeches and interviews since, is one which is unique to him, though grounded firmly in the historic struggles and uprisings of the peasant *pueblos* of Andalusia, and their remarkably deep-seated tendency towards anarchism. These communities are striking for being not just anti-authoritarian, but against all authority. 'I have never belonged to the Communist Party of the hammer and sickle, but I am a communist or communitarian,' Sánchez Gordillo clarified in an interview in 2011, adding that his political beliefs were drawn from a mixture of Christ, Gandhi, Marx, Lenin and Che.

In August 2012 he achieved a new level of notoriety for a string of actions that began, in forty-degree heat, with the occupation of military land, the seizure of an aristocrat's palace, and a three-week march across the south in which he called on his fellow mayors not to repay their debts. Its peak saw Sánchez Gordillo lead a series of supermarket expropriations along with fellow members of the left-communist trade union SOC-SAT.* They marched into supermarkets and took bread, rice, olive oil and other basic supplies, and donated them to food banks for Andalusians who could not feed themselves. For this he became a superstar, appearing not only on the cover of the Spanish newspapers, but across the world's media, as 'the Robin Hood Mayor', 'The Don Quixote of the Spanish Crisis', or 'Spain's William Wallace', depending on which newspaper you read.

---

* The old field-workers' union, the *Sindicato de Obreros del Campo* (SOC), extended its scope to include urban sectors in 2007, giving rise to the Andalusian Workers' Union, *Sindicato Andaluz de Trabajadores* (SAT), within which the SOC maintains a degree of autonomy.

The first time I visited Marinaleda, it was January 2012, and a friend from Estepa had offered to help me get an interview with Sánchez Gordillo. This was arranged not through the usual network of aides and official channels, but through an informal, friendly sequence of favours I would soon learn was entirely typical. My friend Javi called his friend Ezequiel, who lived in the village; Ezequiel wasn't home, so Javi asked Ezequiel's mum, who said of course, she would speak to the mayor when she saw him, and tell him we were dropping by.

So we drove the fifteen minutes from Estepa to Marinaleda, down the hill through undulating olive groves, on a road almost completely free from traffic, around a junction pointing to Marinaleda; someone with delusions of grandeur had scrawled 'ciudad' (city) underneath the village name. We crossed the city limits, which are marked with a painted sign featuring a dove carrying an olive branch and the words 'En lucha por la paz', in struggle for peace. As we slowed down into the main road, we came to a halt at a red light: no one was crossing, and there was no other traffic – it certainly looked peaceful. At first glance, it was difficult to distinguish it from any other Spanish pueblo of this size. The idiosyncrasies don't jump right out at you, but slowly appear and multiply before your eyes, like ants on a hot pavement. It was very quiet. It was very plain. There were no signs indicating multinational brands: no advertising hoardings or intrusions from modern capitalism.

The town hall car park had only a few cars parked in it, the muted sound of children playing drifted over from the nearby nursery, and there, gleaming in the afternoon sunshine, was the Ayuntamiento, the town hall. Next to it was the equally impressive Casa de Cultura, the cultural centre, with its ostentatious pillars painted a brilliant white, framing oblongs of soft blue light on the facade.

Two women were cleaning the steps of the Ayuntamiento, and informed Javi that no, sorry, 'he' is not here right now. A man of about twenty-five in smart jeans, black shirt, black jacket, black stubble and shades emerged, surveying the scene with the confidence unique to those with the good fortune to have both youth and power on their side. This was Sergio Gómez Reyes, one of the village's eleven councillors – later, his face jumped out at us from a wall, on the Izquierda Unida (United Left, IU) election posters. 'If he takes forever to turn up, I'll call his mobile,' Sergio said idly, fiddling with his sunglasses.

So we waited, and kicked our heels in the late afternoon warmth, dark clothes soaking up the dying light, as the shade-line crept diagonally up and over the Ayuntamiento. 'That's his house over there,' Sergio explained, and we toyed with the idea of just knocking on his door. A huddle of women in tracksuit bottoms power-walked down the main road in front of us, gossiping away. In fact, the village is so small that twenty minutes later they were back, going in the same direction on their second lap.

It was so bright that, squinting up at the town hall, I didn't even notice when a man sporting a polyester football jacket and a beard that could topple empires ambled quietly up to the entrance. It was Sánchez Gordillo.

We followed the scourge of Spanish capitalism inside. The lights were off in the foyer – Spanish interiors are often dark, the negative of the brightness outside – but a few posters were still visible on the slightly cracking paintwork: notices of a food bank for the unemployed of neighbouring villages, as well as more commonplace small-town activities like basketball tournaments, photography workshops, and a course on how to use new pesticides. It wasn't exactly palatial – the 'benign dictator' notion perpetuated by more sceptical Spaniards I had met led me to wonder whether the town hall would be adorned with stuffed tigers and comically vulgar paintings.

In the mayor's office the walls were lime green, and the floors cold grey marble: it was very clean, but not at all tidy. His desk was piled with papers and books, a jacket lay discarded on the chair, and scattered on the floor around the edges of the room were cardboard boxes and ring binders, while gifts honouring the town, mostly ceramics, sat proudly on modest bookcases. Where a picture of King Juan Carlos I might normally hang, there was a framed portrait of Che Guevara, declaiming from a podium. Behind Sánchez Gordillo's desk, either side of a framed aerial photo of the town, were a trio of flags slumping dormant on their poles: one bearing the green and white of

Andalusia, one the totemic purple, red and yellow of the Spanish Second Republic (the one Franco launched a coup against, and destroyed, in 1936), and one the green, white and red tricolour of Marinaleda itself.

In the back corner was a flip-chart covered with semi-legible multi-coloured marker pen scribbles, bullet points and wonky arrows; this, it emerged, was the town's budget – that same flip-chart is used when the village is debating its spending and resources at the regular, relatively popular general assemblies. The atmosphere was both dignified and beguilingly amateurish – it felt like what might happen if I suddenly had to run an entire community of 2,700 people. There was a ceiling tile missing, which, living in a world where politicians happily spend £650,000 of public money on their wallpaper, was also rather endearing. We sat on fake leather chairs around a cheap wooden table, rather than facing the desk, which was way too messy for the task at hand. It felt like that was where most of the work got done anyway.

The mayor's zip-up sports jacket had what looked like a small toothpaste stain on the shoulder – the colours were Venezuelan, bold chevrons of red, blue and yellow. It was a homage to Hugo Chávez, who just the day before was on Spanish TV, denying the seriousness of the cancer that would eventually kill him. Sánchez Gordillo had bracelets in blue, green, white, and brown leather on his right wrist, and a solitary red bracelet on the left; it was odd to see a look commonly sported by fifteen-year-old girls in

Camden Market carried off by a swarthy Spaniard in his early sixties. His salt-and-pepper hair was well trimmed, while his beard was a more unruly socialist mess, the kind of beard a Latin American people's hero would be proud of, and that didn't feel like an accident. It was only when he smiled – which he did more and more often, once we had warmed into the interview – that his gappy teeth were revealed in all their glory.

He spoke that day with range and passion, for hours, about the struggle he had led the village through, its general assemblies and hunger strikes, its cultural opportunities and collective personality, and the inhumanity of the capitalist world outside, as well as the misery of its crisis. I left feeling inspired, and slightly dazed, by his stamina, his determination, and indeed his ready willingness to talk about politics for most of the afternoon with some stranger from the other side of Europe, when he probably had better things to do. As the Spanish press realised from their very first encounter with him, during the 1980 hunger strike, Sánchez Gordillo is both an authentic force of nature, captivating, charismatic and persuasive, and a canny user of the media to further the aims of the village, and his own projects.

Afterwards we went in search of a drink. In one of the village's more traditional tapas bars it still felt oddly like the 1970s, decorated sparsely with Blackpool-style comic caricature postcards, and populated by old men quietly nursing their sherries and plates of anchovies. The few children in the bar were drinking Fanta through straws, wearing garish Nike tracksuits like they do everywhere in Spain. But the bar had no signage outside, no branding and no adverts, just a stripy awning.

We popped into the SOC trade union bar, situated in the former town hall, now converted into a social centre, with a large, mural-adorned hall at the back, where the village's general assemblies take place. Twenty-odd men were quietly gabbing away, half-silhouetted, watching the football with one eye, leaning against the cool green tiled columns with small glasses of beer, tossing their olive stones on the floor. Then as night fell we moved on to Palo Palo, the substantial, peculiarly Wild West–themed bar where most of Marinaleda's rock concerts take place, drawing in revellers from across Andalusia. Its wide frontage displays a giant guitar, the body of which is shaped like the map of Andalusia. Inside, there are saloon doors and a fake log effect – it's slightly tacky, but all part of the fun.

Marinaleda is a slender village, comprised of two discrete *barrios* that bulge outwards from one long main arterial road, Avenida de la Libertad: Marinaleda proper, and Matarredonda – though for political and administrative purposes, it is all one *pueblo*. There was once about a kilometre of vacant land between the two settlements, but it is slowly being filled in by the *casitas*, the 350 self-built family homes which constitute one of the village's greatest achievements: the Andalusian regional government provides the materials, the villagers build the houses themselves, and then pay fifteen euros a month as a 'mortgage'.

The first time I explored Marinaleda in daylight, it was in blazing January sunshine, and the village was almost eerily quiet – but then of course it was, as everyone was working. We took a turning off the main street, into a residential street named for José Domínguez 'El Cabrero' – a legendary Andalusian flamenco singer and friend of Sánchez Gordillo's. Many of his songs are about the struggles of the Andalusian *jornaleros*, about the land, about freedom. 'Ah, so he's a socialist?' I asked. 'No! He's a communist!' Javi corrected me, laughing.

El Cabrero wasn't the only one. When Marinaleda's first democratic elections in 1979 returned a majority for Sánchez Gordillo's party, the CUT, or Collective for Workers' Unity, the town council renamed most of the streets. They named one for Fermín Salvochea, the nineteenth-century anarchist mayor of Cadiz, and one for Blas Infante, the 'father of Andalucía', murdered by Francoists for the double crime of being both a regionalist and an anarchist. Plaza de Franco was transformed into Plaza de Salvador Allende, replacing the name of Spain's fascist dictator with Latin America's first democratically elected Marxist leader. There are streets named for fraternity and solidarity, for Federico García Lorca, Che Guevara, and Pablo Neruda, as well as for numerous Spanish communist, republican and artistic martyrs, including the poet Antonio Machado. The man who coined the famous phrase 'the two Spains', describing the secular, progressive left and the more authoritarian, religious right that would fight Spain's Civil War, Machado died in 1939, at the end of the conflict, while fleeing the one Spain he wasn't considered a part of.

If you walk down the wide new boulevard alongside Avenida de la Libertad, you can enjoy an extensive display of well-rendered political murals winding along the white walls. They vary enormously in size, age and quality, but many of them are truly magnificent, and together, they take up a lot of wall space. *Andaluces, levantaos* (Andalusians, arise!), declaims one, alongside the flags of Andalusia and the Spanish Second Republic. Another says 'Turn off the TV / turn on your mind', accompanied by a baby with a TV instead of a head, clutching a euro coin. Slightly less cloying is a painting of the globe, with the seas painted red instead of blue, and a red fist emerging from the north pole, with the robust slogan, 'Against capital – social war!'.

The most striking mural represents a rather different aesthetic to cuddly pacificism (and the village's fondness for doves): alongside a ten-foot-high painting of a hooded man with shadowy eyes is a star, and the slogan *La libertad no se mendiga* – freedom is not begged for. This is a quote from the Cuban revolutionary José Martí, and the second, somewhat more assertive half of the quote is absent from the wall: *Se conquista con el filo de un machete* – it (freedom) is conquered with the blade of a machete.

Other murals call for agrarian reform, demilitarisation, 'peace, bread and work', an end to homophobia, and solidarity either with or from the people of Palestine, Catalunya, the Basque Country, Peru, Vallecas (a working-class district of Madrid) and Colombia – many of them, in fact, were painted by visitors from struggles beyond the village, who came to see what utopia looks like, in the hope they might take a bit of it home with them. The most detailed of the murals depicts the village's notorious land seizures in the 1980s, where they addressed Andalusian land inequality directly by occupying what they deemed to be theirs. A chain of *marinaleños*, Marinaledans, march single file towards the fields in the distance, towards their destiny. They look like L. S. Lowry's figures if they'd been fattened up and bronzed by a Spanish diet and sun.

On the other side of the road is the Estadio Jornalero, the workers' stadium, all painted in the village's ubiquitous tricolour: green for their rural utopian ideal, red for the workers' struggle, white for peace. Directly above the stadium on the hill stands the huge multi-purpose indoor sports pavilion, and immaculately rendered on its wall, looking down on the football stadium and the village, is a painting of Che Guevara's face, approximately the size of a house. Next to this is the *parque natural*, a substantial, well-kept combination of gardens, benches, two tennis courts, an outdoor gym, and a stone amphitheatre where films are screened on hot summer nights. Across the road is the village's outdoor swimming pool – admission costs three euros for the year.

Beyond this hub of sport and leisure possibilities are the village's two schools – one primary, one secondary, and beyond that the *casitas*, the self-built houses. I've never seen a whole street being built on vacant farmland before. It's a strange sensation, and reminds me of the film *Back to the Future*, when Marty McFly is sent back in time to 1955 and comes across the empty stretch of land earmarked to become the street he will one day grow up on, sign-posted only by a dreamy architect's painting.

The new developments in Marinaleda are built directly onto rocky, unpromising black dirt; the darkness on the edge of town is transformed into new life and light. It's a futurist victory, a conquest of sorts – on one half-built street, the shells of the houses are finished and glistening white, but the road is still waiting to be paved, a reminder of the dead dirt before utopia, and the process of transformation: 3-D sketches of utopian lives, blueprints of possibility. Just around the corner is a recently completed street, in sumptuous white.

The process of building is surprisingly straightforward. The Andalusian government provides the basic materials for the new houses, the bricks and mortar, as well as architectural assistance – and then it is up to the residents-to-be, with help from friends, neighbours and comrades, to build them. In theory, the co-operative owns all the houses; in practice, if individual residents want to repaint their homes, or renovate, no one's going to stand in their way. The main point, Sergio explained to me, is to ensure that no one has the opportunity to accumulate capital on their property, and thus to speculate on and profit from the housing market.

It's difficult to argue with this logic, given that you'd be arguing from a position that was instrumental in destroying the Spanish economy. As well as its horrendous eviction stories, crisis-era Spain has four million empty homes, 900,000 of which are new-builds, including entire 10,000-capacity ghost suburbs on the outskirts of Madrid, finished just before the crash and now devoid of life.

While Marinaleda brims with excitement and festivity during its famous annual *ferias* and carnivals, its numerous high-days and holidays, and the rock gigs that see the village momentarily double in size, most of the time it is incredibly peaceful.

Except, an hour or so before dusk, when all hell breaks loose. Dominating the cacophony is a chorus of shrill, chirruping birds. I once asked Antonio, my landlord in the village, what kind of birds they were – he didn't know, but he did a perfect imitation: they sound like a falling bomb in a cartoon, just prior to impact. 'I think they migrated from the park – I think they're tropical?' They're quite difficult to spot because they are clustered tightly in the evergreen orange trees, engaged in fierce but invisible debate.

Competing to be heard are dozens of dogs of diverse size and shape, who have perfected a web-like network of conversation across the white stone garden walls.

In among this come baying cockerels, and from the main road, the slowly grinding gears of a tractor, a few heavy-goods lorries and, with varying regularity, cars pounding out cheaply made dance music, the vehicles' frames rattling along in concert. Because Avenida de la Libertad is also the A-388, connecting other small *pueblos*, such as Herrera and El Rubio, with each other and with the big cities, there's a fair amount of through traffic, kicking up the dust into the hazy sunshine – or, for a few days each winter, the wide, still rain puddles. At the weekend, the through traffic is usually playing reggaeton, the Latin dance music innovation that is surely the most appropriately communist of all dance music subgenres, in the sense that there is seemingly only one rhythm track, without variation, deviation or adornment, available to all its exponents.

One morning, soon after arriving for my first period living in the village, I was invited for coffee with Chris and Ali, two of the ten or so British couples who have retired there (and one of the few who seemed to have done so with an enthusiasm for its political peculiarities). We sat in their back garden in the winter sunshine, and they showed off the work they'd done in their two years there, planting and landscaping. They still needed to buy some garden furniture, they explained, but it was impossible to get across to their Spanish neighbours what garden furniture was. The *marinaleños* couldn't grasp it as a concept – and you can't buy it in the shops. Why? Because the outdoors is for socialising together, publicly: out front, not in the back.

The streets are the social centre of the *pueblo*, observed Julian Pitt-Rivers in *The People of the Sierra*, his landmark 1954 study of the village of Grazalema, only seventy-five miles south of Marinaleda and almost exactly the same size, with a population of just over 2,000.

And sure enough, when the sun is shining, which it almost always is, the older ladies of Marinaleda bring their (dining table) chairs out onto the pavement, together or alone, and chat to their neighbours as they pass by. Alternatively, they take a short stroll to one of the many benches that line Avenida de la Libertad and wait for someone to join them. Front doors are left open, eliding the division between the family space and the public space – even the primary school gates are open while the children play.

To understand Andalusia, its remarkable culture and politics, it is necessary to understand the concept of the *pueblo*. It is a wonderful word which means village, town, or even city, and simultaneously a people – and in that dual meaning lies the key to its magic. A village is its people. You might travel far away from its boundaries, never to return, and subsume yourself into the heady multi-cultures of city life, but you are still, in your essence, a son or daughter of the *pueblo*, and you will never lose that.

Each *pueblo* is a unique space, but its uniqueness comes from the claustrophobia of never being permitted to own, or even roam, the land outside the limits of the village: the unreformed feudal-style system concentrated land ownership in the hands of a few aristocratic families. In the south, the countryside has always been so big and sparsely populated that there is even a social imperative behind the historic congregation in these small communities. The fact Andalusia never had an industrial revolution means there was no great wave of urbanisation in the eighteenth or nineteenth centuries.

For centuries, Andalusian day labourers have settled in these tidily-sized *pueblos*, rather than in big cities or scattered in isolated cottages out in the fields, and this has forged a unique spirit, an ultra-local micro-patriotism, where a *pueblo*'s traditions, idioms and characters are its great strength, and a thriving collective personality develops of its own volition, independent of trends outside. Historically, the Andalusian *pueblo* rejected all authority that derived from outside it. The central state or regional government would often seek to override this, and would often succeed, especially with the Guardia Civil as their sentinels; but the popular desire of a *pueblo* was always for absolute autonomy from outsiders. In fact, Pitt-Rivers cites a third, essentially synonymous definition for the word: *pueblo* meaning 'plebs', an identification of a working-class grouping that separates them from the local rich folk, who 'do not really belong to the *pueblo* but to that wider world which has already been delimited as theirs. In this sense,' he continues, 'the *pueblo* is a potentially revolutionary force.'

It is into this environment that the anarchist philosophy of Bakunin and Kropotkin arrived in the second half of the nineteenth century and found a very congenial home. Theirs was the non-Marxist side of the First International: one that agitated for a working-class revolution and absolute equality, but believed that communism could only be achieved without a centralised bureaucracy, or any hierarchical power structures purporting to act on behalf of the workers. They believed in a federated network of equal but autonomous communities, operating without any interference from centralised power: anarchism described the Andalusian *pueblos* at their most radical, without even meaning to. In this respect, Marinaleda and its political lineage do not represent the communism of the hammer and sickle or Soviet-style centralism.

'The power of elites,' Sánchez Gordillo once said, 'even when they call themselves leftists, is always a tyranny.'

The isolated nature of the Andalusian *pueblos* was even more pronounced in Gerald Brenan's time. In the 1920s and 30s, Brenan spent many years living in the small peasant village of Yegen, in Andalusia's Sierra Nevada mountains, recorded in his classic memoir *South From Granada*. His life there was one of contented detachment. In Yegen's bubble-like totality and de facto self-governance (albeit under the undemocratic leadership of the bourgeois local politicians, the *caciques*), he found both vitality and order:

> This small self-sufficing world had something of the zest for life, and also the sense of measure and balance of the ancient Greeks. When I read in Plato how they had regarded their cities and political constitutions as works of art and had attributed to them not so much moral qualities as aesthetic ones, I thought I understood why this village, which was no smaller than many of the self-governing republics of the Aegean, proved so satisfying.

The result, he records, is that members of the *pueblo* almost never 'left the peasant orbit and became merged in the life of the modern nation'. Politically, the local was everything: the newspapers might report dramatic events in Barcelona or Madrid, but no one in Yegen took the slightest bit of notice – the only news, personalities or politics that counted were those of the village; matters of national life were of no interest. For the Andalusian *pueblos*, Madrid represented a distant, inauthentic power, capable only of misunderstanding, and repressing, their way of life.

This level of isolation and autonomy is of course somewhat diminished in 2013, and in Marinaleda's case, the availability of free wireless internet for all the village is one of Sánchez Gordillo's proudest achievements.

Such techno-positivity is commendable for what remains a small, old-fashioned community, but it might also be its undoing. Modern communications tell of the failures of the capitalist world outside, but they bring the tantalising offer of new possibilities, too. The big regional centres of Seville, Malaga and Granada are enticing some of the young *marinaleños* away from the fields. A few aspire to join the rest of Spain's over-qualified *juventud sin futuro* (youth without a future) and leave the country altogether.

As capitalist Spain sinks (with two general strikes in 2012), it has raised Marinaleda higher than ever above the parapet. Five or ten years ago, when visiting the big cities of the south, I'd expect maybe half of the people I met to have heard of Marinaleda, and maybe half of those to care about it. It was, to many, an amusing Andalusian curiosity, a village of strange rural eccentrics and a testament to the unique political peculiarities of the region. They weren't wrong.

These days, though, everyone in Spain has an opinion on the mayor and his project: it's hard not to, when his face was in the newspapers and on TV every week. Sánchez Gordillo has become akin to what José Bové was in France around the turn of the millennium. Bové is the French farmer and trade unionist who was imprisoned for dismantling a newly-built McDonald's in 1999, in protest at the way the American chain – and capitalism in general – was hurting rural France. He became an icon of the anti-globalisation movement around the time of Seattle, No Logo and the WTO protests, and similarly, Sánchez Gordillo has been catapulted from an entire lifetime of dedicated activism to the dubious status of a celebrity anti-establishmentarian. It is a wonder that the crisis – and the media that must keep the narrative of crisis interesting – has not created more icons of resistance, but one could certainly do worse than the mayor of Marinaleda.

Inevitably, his fame has prompted more press attacks than ever. Marinaleda has long had enemies; as its iconic figurehead, Sánchez Gordillo has survived two assassination attempts, many more attempts at character assassination, and been on trial, and in jail, more times than he cares to count. In the last year the sharks of the Spanish right have circled, growing ever more outraged at the expropriations and occupations. One of the most abstract, but most needling criticisms, is that the village is just 'a communist theme park', where the reality of life is little different from neighbouring villages. In this view the money is leeched from the regional government in Seville, and the self-conscious self-description of the village as 'utopia' really just means rural poverty plus a big painting of Che Guevara's face on a wall.

As the crisis deepens, Sánchez Gordillo worries the elite that Alain Badiou called the 'camarilla of inheritors and parvenus'. He worries them because in a western neoliberal world dependent on resigned submission to TINA – *There Is No Alternative* – he has one, and it seems to work. We may be in a new age of global revolt and assembly, but capitalist realist rhetoric keeps asking the same thing of its dissenters: what's your alternative? It's a rather terse rhetorical question: capitalist language is all about competition, but it doesn't like competitors. From Puerta del Sol to Wall Street to St Paul's, the damning questions rang out: 'What are you *for?* What are your demands? What's your programme? How would it work in practice?'

Marinaleda presents an anti-capitalist answer to those questions, questions that Europe's political and financial elites do not want answered. This community founded on mutual aid and collectivism, not the profit motive, has withstood the global financial crisis far better than its peers: 5 per cent of the town's working population are unemployed, compared to 40 or 50 per cent in many nearby towns – and most of that 5 per cent are recent arrivals who have travelled to 'utopia' in search of work. When all around is misery, Marinaleda offers a glimpse of how things might be otherwise.

Just off Avenida de la Libertad is a metal arch painted in the village's trademark red, white and green, declaiming in capital letters *OTRO MUNDO ES POSIBLE* – another world is possible. I have heard and read this slogan so many times in English, and it usually makes me feel slightly nauseous – it is too often an attempt to fire the imagination that serves only to remind you of the myriad failings of the world you live in. In most parts of the capitalist world, 'another world is possible' is just an idealistic rallying cry. In Marinaleda, it's an observable fact.

Back in January 2012, sitting among the manic clutter of the mayor's office, I asked Sánchez Gordillo about the motto which appears on the town crest, alongside a painting of white houses and a dove against a blue sky. *Una utopia hacia la paz*, it says: a utopia towards peace. He answered:

'We're trying to put in place now what we want for the future. But we don't want to wait till tomorrow, we want to do it today. If we start to do it today, then it becomes possible, and it becomes an example to show others, that there are other ways to do politics, other ways to do economics, another way to live together – a different society.'

He paused, then said the words that drained the capitalist-realist defeatism out of me and carried me halfway back to adolescence.

'Utopias aren't chimeras, they are the most noble dreams that people have. Dreams that through struggle can and must be turned into reality.

'The dream of peace: not the peace of cemeteries, but the peace of equality. As Gandhi said, "peace is not just the absence of violence but the practice of justice": the dream that natural resources and the riches the worker produces will come back to him, instead of being usurped by a minority. At this moment, a few rich people hold the riches that would feed sub-Saharan Africa, that is, 800 million human beings. The dream of equality; the dream that housing should belong to everyone, because you are a person, and not a piece of merchandise to be speculated with. The dream that banks should disappear, that natural resources like energy shouldn't be in the service of multinationals but in the service of the people.

'All those dreams are the dreams we'd like to turn into realities. First, in the place where we live, with the knowledge that we're surrounded by capitalism everywhere; later, in Andalusia and around the world.'

2

The Story in the Soil

*En cada barrio, en cada ciudad, en cada pueblo, en cada
comarca, ahora más que nunca, seguimos en pie.*
[In every district, in every city, in every village, in every
region, now more than ever, we keep standing.]
Poster for 4 December 2012 memorial
to Manuel José García Caparros

Early evening on my first night in Marinaleda, we
pulled up and parked opposite Antonio's house – the
only house in the village where rooms can be rented,
for the princely sum of fifteen euros a night. The front
door was locked and the shutters were down, so we
stood outside on Avenida de la Libertad, wondering
what to do. Slowly a white van crawled towards us,
with two megaphones attached to its bonnet, one
facing right and one left, announcing the same recorded
message over and over again: there would be a general
assembly at 6.30 that evening – half an hour hence, in
fact. In the old days they did the same thing, but

instead of a car, the message was transported around the village on a bicycle.

So we walked the five minutes along the main road to the trade union bar, known as the *Sindicato*, where middle-aged men were pouring themselves whisky from the bottle and chewing sesame seeds. Eventually they drifted through the back door in the bar to the big hall, where the general assemblies take place. It was full, and busy, and bustling with small children to-ing and fro-ing and chirruping, but the meeting was characterised by a sombre tone – the only topic being the serious threat to the farming subsidy the village had come to rely on. Sánchez Gordillo was nowhere to be seen. In any case no resolutions were being proposed or passed; it was just a grim update on how little money was coming in from the regional government in Seville.

The *Sindicato* hall has a large stage for concerts and other performances, but no one was up there. The assembly consisted of some 400 people sitting on fold-out chairs, taking it in turns to grab the microphone at the front, or just shouting out their comments or objections. Above their heads, the permanent backdrop to the stage is a grand painting covering almost the entire wall, depicting three farm labourers boldly striding out from the fields, backed by a whole village of comrades. The contrast between the image and the reality of the situation was the first hint I got that *la crisis* was posing problems for utopia, too. The disjunction between the disquiet in the room and the proud, confident figures in the painting was striking. At the end of the assembly, Councillor Gloria Prieto Buendía, standing in for Sánchez Gordillo, announced in a slightly brighter tone that there were still some seats on the bus leaving in the morning for Malaga, to attend the annual rally for Andalusian workers' liberty and to lay flowers at the shrine to Manuel José García Caparros.

Thirty-five years previously, on 4 December 1977, only two years after Franco died, during the uneasy transition to parliamentary democracy, there were mass demonstrations across Andalusia for regional autonomy. Millions had filled the streets of Spain's largest region, in the cities of Seville, Malaga and Granada, in the towns and in the villages. Caparros, an eighteen-year-old factory worker, attempted to raise the still-banned green-white-green tricolour of Andalusia on Malaga's city council building and was shot dead by the police. Ever since, 4 December has been commemorated in Andalusia, and poor young Caparros has been one of its principal martyrs.

The following morning, twenty or so people climbed onto the bus outside Marinaleda town hall, almost all middle-aged women, chattering away excitably as friends do when on an excursion. It felt a bit like a school outing. Three young men in their late twenties were sitting at the back of the bus, rather more coolly, and there was space at the back, so I joined them there. They were Mosa, one of the village's handful of Senegalese immigrant workers, a tall man with a cheeky smile and a mop of braids; Raúl, a sinewy, stubbly guy who would normally be working in the fields, but had come along to help film the rally, and finally Paco, a dedicated Sánchez Gordillo loyalist who worked for Marinaleda TV and, as I should have guessed from his black hoodie and ponytail, played in the village's premier anarcho-communist ska-punk band (there is only one). In a rather un-*marinaleño* move, the band are called *Molestando a los Vecinos*, which translates as Bothering the Neighbours.

Temperatures had reached the unbearable heights of forty-nine degrees Celsius earlier that year. As we wound south through the Andalusian countryside towards the coast, we passed fields packed with solar panels, huge blue rectangles tilted on stilts, standing in rows like Easter Island statues, folkloric gods saluting the new religion. The Andalusian government has been slow in acknowledging the new reality of unpredictable rainfalls and ever-hotter summers, but the farmers have certainly noticed it – it's already messing with the harvests, and doing so in an economic period when they can ill afford to absorb more disruptive outside influences.

As we passed by the myriad small *pueblos* that populate the south, I showed the young men an obscure old pamphlet I'd found about the village from 1980, entitled *Marinaleda: Huelga de hambre contra el hambre*, the 'hunger strike against hunger' that had taken place before they were born. They flicked through it, amused to see a few familiar faces and names. 'That was the last crisis,' said Raúl. So what comes out of this crisis, I asked – are more Marinaledas possible now? Mosa smiled a sceptic's smile and apologetically demurred – this strange town that he'd come to know and love was a one-off. 'Why should it be?' protested Paco. 'In a town of this size, it is entirely possible. I don't know if it's possible in a big city . . .' The others nodded. 'But if other *pueblos* start their struggle now, imagine what they can be in thirty years' time. It's taken more than thirty years in Marinaleda – that's older than any of us.'

After an hour and a half of idle chit-chat about *la crisis* and football, we were dropped off in Malaga city centre and trooped along in the dazzling winter sunshine to the site of the rally. On a fiendishly windy street corner, the protesters had gathered outside a branch of the BBVA bank, where a large estuary meets a dual carriageway. It was exposed, cold, and very noisy. The green and white flags of Andalusia were already in flight, and individual groups posed with their flowers under a slightly dented metal plaque to the martyr Caparros. Some had wrapped themselves in the flag of SOC-SAT, the left-communist Andalusian trade union representing field labourers since the late 1970s, the union that was the vessel for all of Marinaleda's many struggles and victories.

Raúl and Paco set up the camera on a tripod alongside one local news crew, and the rest of the Marinaleda contingent huddled at the back by a railing. 'We are here in the street to reclaim it for Caparros and the people of Andalusia!' declaimed one in a succession of speakers, drawn from across the region. They seemed unlikely to do so – it was a small event, barely more than 100 people altogether, gathered on the pavement on a chilly Tuesday lunchtime. Wreaths of flowers, tied up with green and white bows, were laid at the foot of the small plaque on behalf of the workers of Malaga, Granada, Marinaleda, Guadalajara and Seville. Despite their heft, the wreaths kept tumbling over in the wind. Marinaleda was by far the smallest conurbation represented, but their wreath was still the biggest and most extravagant. Pieces of paper commemorating Caparros's martyrdom were handed out. He looked so horribly young in the photo, so sadly ignorant of what was to follow that fractious, unstable post-Franco period, and his own senseless death. 'Memory, dignity and struggle', read the injunction at the end.

'Today is not just a day of remembering,' announced Diego Cañamero, the general secretary of SAT, who has so often been Sánchez Gordillo's rabble-rousing partner at big protests and rallies in Andalusia. 'It is also a day for celebrating and looking to the future of our nation.' As he proceeded, Malaga locals pushed through the small throng, trying to go about their business: grumpy-looking old men clinging onto their flat caps, mothers with prams, awkwardly weaving through the crowd.

Because of its size, in a city of 570,000 people, the rally felt terribly niche, but it was no less passionate for that. 'The left must struggle for the future of Andalusia, for the control of its economy in the face of the crisis,' said Cañamero. The traffic continued to roar past behind us, and his voice rose gradually until it was almost a shout, cracking with studied passion and emotion. 'Ninety-nine per cent of the country are fighting for democracy, land and freedom,' he said, and called for a *frente común*, a common front, against the miseries of the crisis. The last time there was an anti-capitalist popular front in Spain was the 1930s, and it was usurped by Franco's coup and the civil war.

The whole event lasted no more than forty-five minutes, and as Cañamero gave an interview to the camera, the crowd melted away into small groups again.

I mentioned to Paco the 1.5 million Catalans who had marched for independence earlier that year. 'Andalusia is different,' he agreed, as we walked back down the dual carriageway in search of our bus. 'It's not like Catalunya, we don't have our own language, or any desire to be independent. But you know we had a Roman civilisation here, and a Moorish civilisation?' He cited the Caliphate of Cordoba with pride. 'Well, I think we have a unique history, and a unique spirit.' He paused. 'How do you say *lucha* in English?' he asked. Struggle, I said, or fight – it depends on the context. 'Well, because that is unique here, too.' He hummed the song that had played at the end of the rally, the crowd standing to attention with fists raised in the air – it was the regional anthem, 'Andaluces, levantaos' (Andalusians, arise). Also known as 'The Hymn of Andalusia', the tune was based on a popular religious song sung in the fields during harvest time. The lyrics, a stirring testament to the Andalusian people, the 'men of light', and their quest for land and freedom, were written by Blas Infante, the father of Andalusian nationalism. It was premiered in July 1936, only a week before the outbreak of civil war, and Infante was executed by the fascists one month and one day after the premiere. It was not revived until after Franco died, and like the flag, the Andalusian anthem became a vital symbol of popular revanchism in the late 1970s: honouring a vociferous liberation movement that had been held back, humbled and brutalised by forty years of fascism. The song paid tribute to a people forever at odds with power, whether it was located in the hands of aristocratic landowners, the Church, the military or Franco's regime. More than anything, the song has become a commemorative tonic for the horrors inflicted on those who had dared to strive to be both Andalusian and free.

For the protesters in Malaga that day, the visible wealth inequalities remain as entrenched now as they ever were. 'Look at the royal family, they're not in crisis,' said Raúl, as we waited beside a cold, sun-bleached roundabout for the bus to take us back to Marinaleda. 'Then look at the rest of Andalusia!' On the pavement next to us, a young couple were huddled with their knees tucked under their chins, begging, with a sign saying they had a three-year-old they could not afford to feed. We talked about the time earlier that year when King Juan Carlos prompted a huge public outcry after going elephant hunting in Botswana – fairly normal behaviour for the Spanish royalty, but that little bit more offensive when 25 per cent of his subjects are out of work, and others are committing suicide rather than be evicted. Spain has always borne witness to these extreme inequalities – and out of that has come some of the most robust popular radicalism seen in European history.

In Andalusia, as in Spain in general, things got better after 1977 – but they did so painfully slowly, and wildly inconsistently. However, once the financial crisis hit in 2008 and sent the construction-driven boom tumbling to its shoddy foundations, most Andalusians were returned to the same struggles for existence they had been fighting for centuries. SOC-SAT's pitch for the rally in Malaga that day was to build 'a popular protest movement as large, determined and united' as that of the post-Franco period, as they outlined in their flyers:

> It is now thirty-five years, two statutes and several constitutional 'upgrades' later, and essentially, we are where we were. Andalusia remains in the rear compared to the other peninsular and island peoples. We continue to be the last in all indices of economic and social welfare. We are first only in unemployment and precariousness, poverty and deprivation.

They blamed this predicament on 'speculative financial capital' and the distant, undemocratic powers in Madrid and Brussels. Those gathered on the windy Malaga intersection spoke of the need to oppose *la dictadura de los mercados*, the dictatorship of the markets: it's a familiar twenty-first-century conjunction – one in which, even so long after the death of Franco, dictatorship was still the preferred word for the situation they endured.

I found it momentarily odd to see this flag-waving coming from people so far to the political left. But then Andalusian nationalism is of an unusual kind – seemingly devoid of chauvinism or parochialism – and its roots lie in the insurgent anarchism of the nineteenth century.

It seems like an astonishing quirk of history, but in 1873, albeit for only two months, Francisco Pi y Margall became leader of the Spanish Federal Republic, a regime of radical decentralisation that sought to replace traditional top-down power hierarchies with horizontal pacts of understanding between free groups and people. As Madrid had promised freedom, in the Spanish country-side, villagers took advantage of the situation to divide up the *latifundios* among themselves and proclaim their pueblos independent sovereign micro-states. Spain briefly became the world's first and only anarchist nation state.

Though a liberal republican and federalist in his politics, Pi y Margall was a friend of the French anarchist thinker Proudhon; among the Spanish poor, support for federalism dovetailed neatly and directly into anarchism. The German writer Helmut Rüdiger, who spent much of the 1930s in Spain, expressed it well when he wrote that

Spanish anarchism is nothing more than an expression of the federal and individualist traditions of the country . . . It is not an outcome of abstract discussions, or theories cultivated by a few intellectuals, but an outcome of a social dynamic force that is often volcanic, and the tendency towards freedom in it can always count on the sympathy of millions of people.

That social dynamic force lies at the heart of Andalusian history, a history littered with poverty and spontaneous, violent uprisings – so when anarchist theory evolved and spread, it found a ready-made support base in southern Spain. In 1871, when the Communist International split between the Marxists, who believed in a strong state, and the Bakuninists, who didn't, Spain was the only country that inclined heavily towards the latter. In Jerome Mintz's anthropological study *The Anarchists of Casas Viejas*, about a tragic failed Andalusian uprising in which many died, we read that 'Bakunin's views matched the Spanish temper – belief in local control and maximum individual freedom – and reflected the Spanish situation – that of an oppressed but potentially explosive rural population.' The forging of a collectivist utopia through protest and land occupation in Marinaleda is not simply a late capitalist story, the exception which ridicules the rule. It's a well-rehearsed rural Andalusian performance of rebellion against a very physical, tangible inequality.

If the dance of popular peasant uprising is innate, the steps practised by the other side are just as entrenched in the Spanish muscle-memory; from the Inquisition, through the brutal repressions of the nineteenth century, into the Civil War, Francoism and beyond, encompassing the 'preventative arrest' and torture of some 20,000 leftists for political crimes in the 1890s, or the dispatching of government troops into factories in Seville to crush worker rebellions. Anticipating the polarity of the Spanish Civil War, revolutionary left-wing groups sought to agitate with ever-greater intensity as the nineteenth century drew to a close; the right-wing authorities were always equal to the task.

Spain is the only country in the world where anarchism ever became a mass movement. The anarcho-syndicalist trade union, the CNT, had over a million members in the pre-Civil War period, a situation which is entirely explicable given the country's economic situation and desperate need for land redistribution. Beyond political context, there is even something anarchist-leaning about the Andalusian personality: individual freedom and mutual aid are both traits held in high esteem – your neighbour is born free to choose his or her own path, but equally, they should not be left to starve if the fates conspire against them.

While for Marx the urban proletariat was the vanguard of revolution, Bakunin's philosophy focused more on a federated network of smaller communities and groups, a conception of communism that already chimed with the lived experience of Andalusian life: the village unit is a self-sustaining ecosystem which regulates itself, and does so without the need for state enforcement, power hierarchies (elected or otherwise) or the desire for profit. For Bakunin, freedom could only come from absolute devolution of power until there was none left at the centre. The 'right of secession' he wrote of was already held to be integral to liberty in the Andalusian *pueblos*. Bakunin called for:

> The internal reorganisation of each country on the basis of the absolute freedom of individuals, of the productive associations, and of the communes. Necessity of recognising the right of secession: every individual, every association, every commune, every region, every nation has the absolute right to self-determination, to associate or not to associate, to ally themselves with whomever they wish and repudiate their alliances without regard to so-called historic rights [rights consecrated by legal precedent] or the convenience of their neighbours.

Of course, the isolated ecosystem of any nineteenth-century peasant village, with its unique customs, assumptions and culture, could make for a challenging environment into which to evangelise. Bakunin warned that their resistance to politicisation would need working around – via a network, connecting the most ready, able, and revolutionary members of each peasant community to talk to one another: 'We must at all costs breach these hitherto impregnable communities and weld them together by the active current of thought, by the will, and by the revolutionary cause.'

Bakunin was writing about rural Russia, but 'hitherto impregnable communities' is the perfect description of the Andalusian *pueblos* of the nineteenth century. While they may have been somewhat culturally hermetic, some of their inhabitants did at least leave home, usually the men; thousands of workers were regularly compelled to travel great distances to find work, in order to survive. Most itinerant Andalusian day labourers migrated to the cities and emerging industries of the north, especially Catalunya and the Basque Country; others went elsewhere in rural Spain, or to France – wherever seasonal farm work was most plentiful. There, sleeping on barn floors for months at a time with scores of other poor labourers, revolutionary ideas were easily shared.

Among Spain's many regions, anarchism thrived most of all in rural Andalusia (with a strong uptake in urban Catalunya, for different reasons). And yet, Andalusia is not the only poor part of Spain, far from it – parts of Extremadura and Castile, for example, have long been desperately poor. As Temma Kaplan writes in *Anarchists of Andalusia 1868–1903*, it is actually the contrasting wealth, not poverty in itself, which explains the region's innate radicalism: 'Where almost everyone is poor, the idea of revolutionary social changes might seem utopian, for if everything were equally divided, everyone would be equally poor.' It is the visible wealth inequalities in the south which have made it so susceptible to radical ideas.

'Andalusia is not a poor country,' wrote the authors of the Marinaleda hunger strike pamphlet in 1980, 'it was made poor.' Likewise, they argue, it was made revolutionary by the behaviour of outsiders. By seeking to impose a uniform Spanish culture on the regions, to create 'one Spain' under God and under the King, remote bourgeois centralism fomented the revolutionary atmosphere of the nineteenth and early twentieth centuries. Looking back over Andalusian history, they write, 'there are constants of oppression, and there are constants of struggle'. Positioned against the ordinary people of the *pueblos* were *gran propietaria*, big property, identified as the bourgeoisie, the aristocracy and the Catholic Church – with the Guardia Civil as their hired thugs and the corrupt *caciques* as their political representatives. *Gran propietaria* has a contemporary equivalent, as the nature of capitalist exploitation has changed: on demonstrations in 2013, the oppressors, when identified in one phrase, are *gran capital*, big business.

Electoral politics has rarely offered the poor labourers of Andalusia much hope of a solution. There was a pretence of democracy in the late nineteenth and early twentieth century, via the election of local *caciques* – normally a choice between two bourgeois men of means: a conservative or a nominal liberal; the latter distinguishable only by the mildest of anti-clericalism. Even when anarchism began to flourish in the south, the sheer desperation of the landless labourers impelled them to keep voting for these men. The *caciques* looked after the interests of the land-owners, and coercion, buying votes and electoral fraud were commonplace, as was intimidation from the local members of the Guardia Civil. The *caciques'* men chose the shift workers from those assembled in the town square, and, quite simply, if you wanted the miserly amount of work on offer you had to vote the way they commanded.

The tension in Spain between the big central state and the miniature world of the *pueblo* preceded Franco, and even Primo de Rivera, the country's proto-fascist dicta-tor from 1923–30. There has long been a sense of a distant, imposing political class who do not understand the local ways and needs of each *pueblo*, in their many and varied forms. It's the same rhetoric you might hear in American election races about Washington, D.C., the remoteness of power, both geographically and in terms of its comprehension of local realities. Centralism, wrote the *marinaleños* behind the hunger strike pamphlet, is 'the origin of all our old problems, since the end of the nine-teenth and across the twentieth century, and the cause of all our riots, our demands, and our revolutionary move-ments.' Struggle, they continue, is the heritage of the Andalusian people – *un pueblo combativo*, a pugnacious people, and the methods (crop burnings, strikes, land occupations) have long been the same, as has the enemy on the ground, the Guardia Civil, with their 'centuries in the service of the landowners'.

In the towns of Andalusia, wrote Gerald Brenan in his classic 1943 text *The Spanish Labyrinth*, 'the atmosphere of hatred between classes has to be seen to be believed. Since the Republic came in, many landlords have been afraid to visit their estates. And the labourers are all Anarchists. What else can one expect under such conditions – miserable pay, idleness for half the year and semi-starvation for all of it?' The *jornaleros*, the day labourers of villages like Marinaleda, lived without smallholdings or allotments to grow food for basic family subsistence during the six months they were without work. Without credit from the shops of the *pueblo* during the lean times, or the gift of a loaf of bread from one's neighbours now and then, even more would have died of malnutrition.

While the *jornaleros'* poverty was often fatal, hundreds of thousands of acres of the aristocratic-owned arable lands around them were left uncultivated, adding greater insult to the labourers' injurious poverty. These lands were sometimes used for breeding bulls or horses, or in the case of a 56,000-acre tract of land west of Marinaleda, simply as a shooting estate. The class hatred flowing in one direction was matched only by the disinterest flowing in the other. Brenan records a visit in the 1930s by the Duke of Alba, father of Marinaleda's nemesis, the current *duquesa*, to some of the vast lands he owned in Andalusia. He arrived, wrote Brenan, 'with an equipment of lorries and tents, as though he were travelling in the centre of Africa'.

Meanwhile, starving labourers who attempted to plough the fallow land were beaten by the police.

Estepa, Marinaleda's nearest moderately-sized neighbour, with a population of 12,000, is famous for three things: biscuits, bandits and mass suicide. The biscuits in question are Christmas delicacies called *mantecados*, and every winter entire buses are chartered from Seville and Malaga, filled with people eager to stock up for the festive season. *Mantecados* (pronounced *man-teh-cow* in the impenetrable local accent) taste a bit like grenades of sugared dirt, and weigh about the same. And yet, it's not Estepa's confectionery that lingers longest in the stomach. In the year 208 BC, the residents of what was then a small but significant hilltop outpost of Carthage saw the Roman army in the distance, coming to seize the town. By the time the Romans arrived, every last citizen of Estepa was dead – the whole population had committed suicide rather than surrender. The town was later captured by Visigoths, and then by a series of rival Moorish caliphs, followed eventually by the Christian *Reconquista*.

One day, Javi and I took a walk up Estepa's San Cristóbal hill to look at its multicultural relics, our toes tensing to grip the harsh gradient, feeling the cobbles as we climbed through and above the town itself. The final stretch of the hill was so steep that my lungs took a beat to catch up, and even in the relative chill of January, tiny beads of sweat grew on my forehead, immediately turning cold in the breeze. There was no one at the top, and no wind either. The church tower was a fancy peach-coloured extravagance, a bohemian cake of a building drawn straight from an Aesop's fable.

The view from here is known as the *Balcón de Andalucía,* the Balcony of Andalusia. Here you can see Marinaleda to the north, on the gentle slope down towards the great Guadalquivir River that brings life to the otherwise parched region. The river was once the glittering conduit for masses of Spanish gold violently plundered from the New World. Estepa looked especially pretty, with its staggered cascade of white walls and red roofs falling away down the hill beneath us, poised delicately above the regiments of endless olive groves and rich green fields dulled by the orange pastel-dust.

This land, the basin of the Guadalquivir, is often dry, but not unfertile: as with all of rural Andalusia, it is concentrated in very few hands – either the aristocratic families of old Castile, or the middle classes, who took the opportunity in the nineteenth century to buy up (at low cost) terrain that had previously been common or Church lands. '*¡Corazón de Andalucía!*' proclaimed the signage of a disused hotel on the edge of Estepa, with the unselfconscious pride of a flamenco dancer flicking her castanets. This is indeed the heart of the region: you're a pretty long way from anywhere, but you can see *everywhere.*

We stood on a wooden viewing platform and watched the dark close out on Estepa below us. From here you can see three sub-regions of Andalusia – Seville, Cordoba and Granada – and amid the fields, the sparsely-scattered *pueblos* in the distance: El Rubio, Casariche, Herrera, and Marinaleda itself. Of course, at that distance these small farming communities all look the same. So much that is in them *is* the same: children kicking cheap footballs against stone walls worn down by the centuries, Cruzcampo umbrellas dozing gently outside tapas bars. And yet, like Asterix's village in Gaul, impossibly holding out against the Romans, Marinaleda is surrounded by villages that lie in enemy hands.

It's an area which, because of its often desperate levels of poverty, has long given itself to people's heroes, for good or ill. And before the anarchists and communists arrived, there were the *bandoleros*, the bandits – normally involved in smuggling, extortion, and highwayman-style hold-ups. Even the bandits, writes Kaplan, 'were a friend of the poor and its champion against its oppressors . . . a safety-valve for popular discontent'. There are even tours celebrating this grisly part of local history – though where the likes of El Tempranillo, El Pernales or El Lero fit on a spectrum of malevolence from Robin Hood to Jack the Ripper depends on who you speak to. These weren't true popular heroes, Javi explained to me. They were horrendous murderers, living in defiance of the law and using the masses as human shields against the authorities.

In the face of such danger, the Guardia Civil, or para-military police force, was founded in the mid-nineteenth century for the express purpose of tackling banditry in this part of Andalusia. The local landscape was the bandits' friend. Late one cold February night, driving back towards Estepa from a pre-Lenten *carnaval* in another town, Javi and his friend Antonio explained that the tree-covered hills were considered too dangerous for exploring alone – there was a white dog in there that would eat you alive. This is presumably where the bandits used to hide, too, I asked – a slightly more realistic danger? 'That's right,' said Javi. Antonio chuckled to himself from the back seat.

'The *bandoleros* would probably still be there, too – but it's so fucking cold, they had to come down the mountain and get jobs in Congress.'

Spanish hills are usually concealing something, even if they have sometimes been sites of salvation: havens for rebel peasant leaders hiding from persecution, and for the Spanish *maquis*, the partisan guerrillas who didn't give up on the dream, even after the fascists won the Civil War in 1939, and fought on against Franco. The partisans are the people's heroes depicted in the Oscar-winning film *Pan's Labyrinth*, a ragtag army refusing to be cowed by the greater power intent on destroying them, deployed in the three branches of the Spanish State: the military, the Church and the government.

Like the bandits, anarchists in hiding from the authori-ties took cover in the Andalusian hills – sometimes for years on end, avoiding arrest and execution by the Guardia Civil. In fact, the different outlaws helped each other: the bandits concealed in the hill towns and the mountains made it easier for revolutionaries and fugitives, as well as cloth and tobacco smugglers, to move their intellectual or commercial wares in secrecy, sneaking on foot over narrow mountain ridges to the next town.

When itinerant evangelical preachers were spreading anarchism through the countryside in the late nineteenth century, it was known simply and magnificently as 'the idea'. The Andalusian river valleys became its conduits, carrying newspapers, people and 'the idea' from town to town – a red and black river through the blanched, dusty fields. It travelled with astonishing speed in Spain, 'carried from one village to the next by Anarchist "apostles"', writes Brenan in *The Spanish Labyrinth*. They travelled light and cheap, 'like tramps or ambulant bullfighters under the tarpaulins of goods wagons', and received no pay or retainer, instead living 'like mendicant friars on the hospitality of the more prosperous work-men'. Anarchists were poor: Bakunin himself couldn't afford the train fare to Barcelona for the inaugural congress of his own branch of the International, but his lieutenants made up for their impecuniousness with fervour. The campaign was kept alive through newspapers such as *El Socialismo* and *El Productor*, often sold via the barber. *El Productor* even had local agricultural correspondents in the south, to report on the increasingly violent uprisings in the region.

Fermín Salvochea, known as the 'saint' of Spanish anarchism, edited some of these papers, including *El Socialismo*, which helped bring Kropotkin's ideas to the peasants of the south. A nineteenth-century Sánchez Gordillo, he later became an icon for the *marinaleños*. When he wasn't busy being in jail or leading armed uprisings against the Spanish state, he served as mayor of Cadiz, in the late nineteenth century; even before universal suffrage, it was possible to get to the top in Andalusian local government while opposing the idea of hierarchical power. Fifty thousand people attended his funeral in 1907, an event worthy of the beatification of a more religious kind of saint. There is, of course, a street named after him in Marinaleda.

More often than not, the struggles of the valiant sons and daughters of Andalusian workers' rebellion resulted in failure. The repeated uprisings were crushed, thanks to the landowners' military henchmen in the Guardia Civil. In 1884 seven peasants were executed in Jerez de la Frontera – 100 miles south-west of Marinaleda – for their alleged involvement in a secret group called *La Mano Negra*, The Black Hand, the infamous anarchist terrorist organisation whose existence may or may not have been entirely invented by the state. *La Mano Negra* had been blamed for a series of murders and acts of arson in the preceding years. As a result, whether the allegations were fictional or not, the anarchist press was banned and some of its leading lights forced into hiding.

The mythology stuck around. 'The shadow of *La Mano Negra*, the secret and righteous brotherhood of the last century, looms over the plazas of Andalusia's villages and runs through its farms', began an article in the generally sane national newspaper *El País* in 1981. The ostensible subject of the article, beyond reviving the far-left bogeymen of a century before, was the burgeoning activities of Sánchez Gordillo's field-workers' union, the SOC. Sensationalism aside, *El País* was at least correct to acknowledge the 'common tradition', and that Andalusian *jornaleros* 'have not forgotten what constitutes their past, nor what they experienced, nor what has been handed down from father to son'. And what were they doing with that shared history of starvation, brutality, torture and repression? Working on revenge.

3

La Lucha

*We want peace. The people always wanted peace. But be
clear that we do not want the peace of the last forty years of
gazpacho, lice and cortijos,* or all that which is preached by
the Pharisees of the old established disorder.*

Juan Manuel Sánchez Gordillo, 'Hunger and Peace',
El País, 1982

We arrived at El Humoso and parked the car. It was a mild,
misty January day, the sunlight gleaming through the
hanging mist. The air tasted as clean as water, and the only
sounds disrupting this rural idyll were the odd rooster in
the background and a dog barking at nothing in particular.
On one side of the car park was a large olive oil processing
factory, on the other a freshly painted white farm adminis-
tration building, adorned with a red roof, its windowsills
and columns picked out in green. It looked like a mansion
house from America's old South, *détourné* by its paint job

---

* A *cortijo* is a prosperous farm, grange or ranch, its compound often
enclosed by a wall.

in the Marinaleda colour scheme. To the side stood large greenhouses for tomatoes, spinach and lettuces, supplementary crops to be sold in the town's grocery shops. The entrance to the fields was marked by a giant single-wall facade plastered with two substantial political murals.

'*Este cortijo es para los jornaleros en paro de Marinaleda*' (this farm is for the unemployed labourers of Marinaleda) was written in massive capital letters along one stretch of wall, punctuated with a painting of the village's iconic tricolour flag. On the other side was a giant socialist-realist painting of two fifteen-foot tall *jornaleros* emerging proudly, tired, from their work in the fields, with *TIERRA UTOPIA* written underneath.

A family lives on the El Humoso farm as caretakers, running the day-to-day operations; but they are neither bosses nor owners – this is a co-operative, my guide stressed. This is *the* co-operative, in fact: the symbolic and actual cornerstone of Marinaleda's utopian achievement – a 1,200-hectare farm won through thirteen years of relentless struggle. In 1991 the land was expropriated from the Duke of Infantado (in exchange for an undisclosed sum in compensation) and awarded by the Andalusian regional government to the people of Marinaleda.

We walked over to the farm's olive oil processing plant, where four or five men in blue overalls were operating the machinery. The olives are stripped from any twigs by the first machines, then cleaned by blasts of water, then smashed into pulp. From this mash the gooey oil is siphoned off, then filtered, and filtered again. The collective produces 300,000 litres of olive oil a year. Scattered around the gleaming pipes and machinery were boxes stamped with the Marinaleda *Cortijo* El Humoso logo, in red, white and green, and a stamp of the same *tierra utopia* painting from the farm.

The stock room felt like an ersatz version of big-C Communism: identical piles of boxes, stacked high, all bearing the farm logo; a colour-coded livery of plenty. Before it's bottled, the olive oil is stored in giant cylindrical silos, and even there the Marinaleda aesthetic is evident: the floor is green, the walls are white, the measuring sticks on the side of each silo are red. Outside, the factory walls themselves, and even the little pavement around the edge of the building are painted in the tricolour: the ubiquity of the colour scheme makes the farm and the oil factory feel like a sports stadium complex – indeed, it makes fidelity to the village, and the project, feel like supporting a football team.

Antonio Sánchez actually looked like a character from Asterix – tall, broad and fit despite his advancing years, with a big bushy moustache. At times it feels like every third person in Marinaleda is called Antonio, and so he is known as *El Bigotes*, 'the whiskers'. He has worked in the oil factory for all of its twelve years in existence, and before that was a town hall employee for twenty years – ever since the struggle began in 1979. He's been close to Sánchez Gordillo since the beginning. He briefly lived in Cordoba in the 1970s, migrating to the city for work like so many others, but returned when the struggle began.

Those first few years, Antonio recalled with a big grin that disturbed his moustache, were a red-hot period, a boiling point. Diving back into those formative memories, he transmitted a similar excitement to that I've seen on the faces of young members of Spain's *indignados*: the intense thrill that comes from determinedly standing together against the status quo and announcing you are going to make something new. The ineffable, irrepressible subjectivity of solidarity.

We talked about the land seizures, the hunger strikes, the arrests, the tireless years of struggle which at last earned them the farmland that stretched beyond our view for miles. This was a struggle that brought not just work to the people of Marinaleda, but life to 1,200 hectares (close to five square miles) of idle fields. Antonio seemed quite pleased to talk about the old days; unlike Sánchez Gordillo, his job does not regularly involve recounting tales of yesteryear, certainly not to foreign journalists. It was never as simple as just one occupation, he explained; in fact they had to occupy these very fields over and over again – the *marinaleños* would be arrested, sometimes imprisoned or beaten, and then they'd regroup and start over again.

'The Guardia Civil would be here, defending the Duke. Look at the trees,' he gestured, his arm casting a long shadow beneath the low-lying winter sun. There was a line

of leafless, sorry-looking trees lining the path from the main road into El Humoso, which appeared to have been not so much pruned as amputated. 'When we first came here to protest it was the summer, and very, very hot. The Guardia Civil cut the tree branches off, so we would have no shelter.' With normal summer temperatures around forty degrees, removing the only natural source of shade in sight is evil genius worthy of a cartoon villain. He shook his head; the memory still burned through. 'They wanted us to give up and go home.'

In those early days, to work on 'the project' together, trying to create utopia from scratch after decades of dictatorship and centuries of poverty, was the only option. It was, the veterans say now, necessary just to survive. For all that *la lucha* was bred out of misery and hopelessness, it fired their synapses, it was thrilling – a release of that unique kind of energy you can only get from knowing you are fighting for a just cause. And that maybe – just maybe – you might win.

Before tracing *la lucha* itself, it's worth recapitulating the historical background: the Spanish left had had a democracy – even a revolution, perhaps – snatched away from them. In 1931's general election, left-wing parties of all varieties thrived, the monarchy was banished, and on 14 April that year, the Spanish Second Republic was declared. But in rural areas this was a victory without gains – it did not in itself herald a new era of the one thing that could stabilise rural Spain and feed its people: agrarian reform, and land redistribution.

The prospect of land and freedom suddenly appeared tantalisingly close, and yet the reality was still sorely lacking. As a result, rural Spain witnessed intense, frequent peasant mobilisations, land seizures, clashes and strikes. In Gilena, a *pueblo* ten miles from Marinaleda and about the same size, there had been no voting, because the socialists had been barred from standing by a corrupt *cacique* who was also a landowner. Increasingly disgruntled as the summer wore on, in October 1931 the infamous Gilena Events took place. What began with a general strike quickly degenerated into confusion, a heavy-handed response, stand-offs, a stolen gun, rapid escalations on both sides: the upshot was one dead Guardia, five dead workers, and fifty injured.

It was not the only such tragedy, or even the worst. Casas Viejas was yet another Andalusian *pueblo* the size of Marinaleda, with the same composition of desperate, landless labourers, further inflamed by their new anarchist faith. In January 1933 there were anarchist uprisings in Barcelona, Madrid and Valencia, which were quickly suppressed, but news of their failure did not reach Casas Viejas in time. Believing the revolution had finally arrived, armed workers surrounded the local Guardia Civil barracks; there was an exchange of fire, and two of the guards were killed. Reinforcements were sent in, the village was occupied, and a massacre ensued. The

beatings, reprisals, and a siege-via-fire resulted in a total of twenty-eight deaths over the following forty-eight hours.

As with Gilena, the tragic events of Casas Viejas prompted soul-searching and recriminations on a national scale — but while they were shocking, they were neither isolated nor, in retrospect, surprising. There were 238 strikes in Seville province between the declaration of the Second Republic in 1931 and the outbreak of the Civil War with Franco's coup in 1936. The anarchist trade union, the CNT, called their actions in this period 'revolutionary gymnastics'. And like all gymnastics, the flexibility, strength and spontaneity of the workers' uprisings were only possible thanks to long periods of training.

The promise of the pre-Civil War period dissolved in the relentless horrors of the conflict itself and the brutal vengeance of Franco's White Terror that followed the fascist victory in 1939. It was a revolution not only delayed, but, by necessity, forgotten. The rallying cry of agrarian reform, the only solution to the volatility, hunger and misery of life for the landless labourers of Andalusia, went unheeded. After the Civil War, and for the best part of four decades of fascist dictatorship, the land surrounding the impoverished *pueblos* remained as it always had been, in the hands of the aristocratic houses of Infantado and Alba.

By the time Franco died, during a period in which most of their European counterparts were enjoying the fruits of technological, social and cultural progress, the *jornaleros* of Andalusia could reasonably consider their lot and observe that it had barely improved in almost 200 years.

Franco died in November 1975, at the age of eighty-two; his funeral was attended by such luminaries as General Pinochet and the Bolivian dictator Hugo Banzer. Spain breathed a long-overdue sigh of relief and embarked upon *la Transición*, awkwardly loosening the chains of dictatorship. The words of the Franco-era Spanish national anthem, *La Marcha Real*, full of the patriotic bombast that characterises most national anthems, were removed in 1978. As a mark of the tense uncertainty of the period, nothing was put in their place – indeed, to this day, Spain's national anthem is one of only two wordless anthems in the world.

It was clearly going to take some time to recover from the brutality – indeed, the sheer abnormality of living in a fascist dictatorship for three decades after the end of World War Two. To make matters worse, Franco had also left the Spanish economy in a terrible mess. The south was particularly hard-hit. The little capital raised in Andalusia from farming, mining or fishing invariably ended up invested or hoarded elsewhere in the country, amid chronic underinvestment. Dictators do not have to worry about regions falling massively behind, especially when the citizens of those regions were on the wrong side in a civil war and had a history of anarchism and anticlericalism.

'The famous centres of Francoist development were demagogic castles', wrote the authors of *Huelga de Hambre*, 'created to fill the pages of newspapers – and the pockets of a handful of speculators and political junkies of the regime.' Andalusia was left lamentably under-developed. The land was mostly idle, industry was almost non-existent, and there were severe shortages of teachers and school places and high levels of illiteracy. It was only the new tourist developments on the Costa del Sol which offered any work in the construction industry – and even then, the profits rarely stayed in the region. The poverty in rural areas was so dire that, as late as the 1970s, children would frequently have to abandon their schooling to work in the fields, when there was work, or migrate with their parents to find seasonal work in other parts of Spain. There had been *una riada humana*, a human flood, away from the *pueblos*. So bad had the farming situation become that 3 million Andalusians emigrated in the 1960s.

Juan Manuel Sánchez Gordillo was born in Marinaleda in February 1949 and was still in his mid-twenties when the struggle began. 'When I was growing up,' he told me, 'it was a village of migrants. They would go to Germany or France; or for two months a year to the wheat fields in the north to look for work. Otherwise they were unemployed. There was utter destitution. The surroundings were all huge expanses of private land. Next to what is now the highway there's the land of a Marquis. Then on the way to Seville there are other *cortijos* belonging to the

Duchess of Alba.' These are the *latifundios*, the mega-estates.

The land itself, Sánchez Gordillo wrote in his 1980 book, *Marinaleda: Andaluces, levantaos*, is the centre of gravity in Andalusia, for 'it is on the land that the future will be built'. He was fond of comparing the situation of Andalusian peasant towns to that of Native American reservations, where native tribes driven from the plains where once they dwelt and worked are contained in miserable isolation, surrounded by the land which belongs to them – producing and reproducing poverty, humiliation and cultural degradation. He records one fellow *marinaleño* approaching him 'crying like a child' in the late 1970s and telling him: 'Juan Manuel, I'm not a beggar. I want a job, because I am fifty-four and ashamed to be anywhere else than working in the fields'.

The demonstrations had begun before Franco died, as the increasingly desperate people of the south gained confidence – confidence in the absence of any hope of change from above. The familiar Andalusian dialectic of rebellion and repression intensified in the early 1970s, with huge construction industry demonstrations in Granada and strikes – which were still illegal – throughout the middle period of the decade, as well as sporadic crop burnings on the nobles' estates. The Guardia Civil continued to exert the violence they had used in the nineteenth century and during the Civil War, and there were a number of deaths on demonstrations. For the impoverished

Andalusian *jornaleros*, the death of *el Generalísimo*, though it did not itself guarantee the liberal democracy that would eventually follow – the first free general election was in 1977 – was a clear opportunity to raise the game. It was a classic crisis-opportunity.

As the tensions of the constitutional Transition proceeded, Marinaleda began working on, and towards, its own definition of freedom. Before the land seizures, before the collective farm, before economic democracy, before the virtually free housing, before the assassination attempts, before the supermarket raids, before utopia – came organisation. The rage of the strikes and demonstrations of the 1970s was bundled into the foundations of a movement. In 1976 the field workers' union, the *Sindicato de Obreros del Campo* (SOC) was founded, and soon after the Marinaleda chapter formed in the garden of what is now Avenida de la Libertad. It was to be a union for day labourers, focusing on direct action, with a broadly anarchist philosophy. It was designed to be responsive to the precarity of the Andalusian peasant existence. At that time, Spanish union law prohibited voting in union elections until you had worked for the same employer for more than six months – ruling out 98 per cent of the 500,000 Andalusian field workers, severing an entire class from labour organisation.

On 4 December 1977 young Caparrós was martyred, and the following January, the SOC began occupying the land. Early the following year, SOC's Marinaleda chapter occupied a farm twenty miles away, near Osuna, for two days – the first time they had done so since the Second Republic. It ended when they were violently evicted by the Guardia Civil and several union leaders were jailed.

Meanwhile in Madrid, a new democratic Constitution had been written. In Marinaleda they held a general assembly to discuss it, and an official position was decided on: they would abstain from voting in the referendum to approve the Constitution. Most of the *pueblo* were already involved in the occupations and strikes, and wished to continue focusing their democratic energies that way. (They have maintained this ambivalence: in the context of the current Spanish crisis, I have heard the Constitution described in Marinaleda as a 'pact with the residues of Francoism'. In their propaganda, it is accused of being 'useless in stopping the markets' war against the people'.)

They had chosen to ignore the new developments in Madrid, but Madrid had nonetheless noticed them. The Andalusian workers worried the Spanish bourgeoisie, a class largely composed of Francoists surreptitiously changing out of their uniforms. With some alarm, the Madrid newspapers quoted one of SOC's founders as claiming that 'the labourers, in essence, are anarchists at heart'. Suddenly, without the sanctions of Franco's dictatorship to protect landed interests, the labourers' union embodied a cathartic release of long-suppressed tension. Its philosophy was both radical and apparently disinterested in Soviet or Leninist dogma.

From the outset the *marinaleños* 'declared the sovereignty of food', as Sánchez Gordillo explained it to me, asserting that 'food was a right and not a business; that agriculture should be out of the World Trade Organisation; that natural resources should be at the service of the communities that work them, and who use them'. While he has long expressed global solidarity for any marginalised community, and a corollary hatred of Western imperialism and militarism, it is the local needs of the *pueblo* that matter most. From the outset, sovereignty of the crops, and sovereignty of the terrain to grow them in, was the central tenet of the Marinaleda philosophy. Land, went the slogan, is a gift of nature, like air or water.

Then as now, Sánchez Gordillo had a gift for making the revolutionary sound like basic common sense. 'Property', he wrote in *Andaluces, levantaos*, 'has no reason to exist when not serving a social purpose. To abolish property is not radicalism when that property produces hunger and scarcity for so many.'

As a partner organisation to SOC, this burgeoning *jornaleros* movement established a political party, in 1979 forming the *Colectivo de Unidad de los Trabajadores* (CUT): an explicitly anti-capitalist political party, positioned to the left of the Communist Party of Spain. That year, the first free local elections since the Second Republic and the Civil War were held. The CUT won 76 per cent of the vote in Marinaleda (the centre-right coalition UCD the remaining 22 per cent), and thus nine of the eleven councillors for the village's municipal council. They have maintained an absolute majority on the council ever since.

The CUT is not a traditional communist party, according to any tradition understood outside the region. It is neither a regular Marxist-Leninist party, nor a Trotskyite or Maoist one. 'Our union gathers people of many political stripes,' Sánchez Gordillo explained to me, 'but we carry the torch of anarchism's direct action. Even the assembly is direct action.' He went on to cite 5,000 years of Andalusian struggle for land as the psychic engine of his movement. This lineage is more important to the CUT and SOC philosophy than 1789, 1848 or 1917.

Even while participating in the standard Spanish electoral processes, Marinaleda's relationship with representative democracy is unique. 'When we got to the city council we realised we had to transform power – that the power that had previously worked to oppress could not also work to liberate.' He calls this 'counter-power', an inversion of the existing pyramid: 'the power of poor people against the power of the rich. For this counter-power to be effective, we realised that participation was fundamental. This is why we organised everything around an assembly – an assembly that was open to all workers, regardless of political affinity.'

For him, traditional power structures are incapable of helping the poor, as well as unwilling. One *pueblo* participating and reaching decisions together will make fewer mistakes than a single leader or group, Sánchez Gordillo told me – and even when they do, which they do, they are at least accountable to themselves. Their realisation in those early days, he wrote in 1985, had been that 'laws, customs, officials, habits, budgets, regulations and standards of the Ayuntamiento' were all instruments of power, 'helpful to fascism, but useless as a tool of struggle and freedom for the people. That old machinery had to be destroyed.'

The assemblies became the heart of village life in the 1980s, and as a consequence, the heart of the struggle. These days they are normally attended by an average of 200–400 *marinaleños* and take place sporadically throughout the year. There should be approximately one per week, but it depends on what needs discussing, and how pressing it is. This 'direct democracy', with simple 'hands-up' voting, is where a great deal is discussed and decided: the budget for the town council, local rates and taxes, the election of political posts within the town, and resolutions to mobilise for more direct action.

After a decade of strikes and burgeoning labourer organisation, one event took place that drew the world's attention to Marinaleda for the first time and became the definitive event in establishing the village's place in modern Spanish history. In August 1980, against a backdrop of strikes across the region, Marinaleda hosted the 'hunger strike against hunger' – *una huelga de hambre contra el hambre*, in which 700 people refused food for nine days.

'Our struggle', Gordillo said then, 'arises in a time when the socioeconomic situation has reached unbearable extremes.' The village was in a truly desperate state by the summer of 1980. In the first seven months of the year they had received an equivalent of 200 pesetas per family per day – less than two euros. At best, most of the *jornaleros* could afford to buy only lentils, rice, onions and tomatoes from the village shops. Going two days without food so the children could eat was common, as was community solidarity: where families could share their food with one another, they did.

One story I'd heard, about a group of neighbours clubbing together to buy a gas cylinder for a family of nine to see them through the winter, was met with nods of recognition when I repeated it to other older *marinaleños*. That was just what you did. The week the hunger strike began, the Guardia Civil had taken nine men from Marinaleda to the police station after finding them foraging for sunflower seeds in the fields. When Sánchez Gordillo described the poverty among landless labourers in Andalusia as a 'social holocaust', this was the kind of thing he had in mind.

Their demand upon launching the hunger strike was for an increase in 'community employment funds' (essentially, paid public-works projects for the unemployed) – but this was only a short-term solution, enough to sustain them until the olive harvest came in December. The community employment funds did nothing to address the root causes of the poverty, simply subsidising and stabilising a miserable status quo with humiliating, pointless work like cleaning ditches – which in any case could be done much faster by machines. What was needed was what had always been needed: substantial land reform.

This, they argued, could be achieved through a change in the crop management of the 23,000 hectares of land between Herrera and Écija, which were planted with labour-light dry crops like corn and sunflowers. The Marinaleda proposal was to sow crops that created substantially more work, like tobacco, cotton or sugar beet, and to create secondary industries for processing them. This, they argued, would instantly lead to a 30 per cent reduction in unemployment in central Andalusia. They also proposed the reforestation of some of the village's environs with almond and pine trees, and the construction of a dam on the Genil River to irrigate the 50,000 hectares of arid land around it.

Their demands, and their actions, were discussed and ratified by daily general assemblies, with even the children voting – because some of them, too, had volunteered to take part in the hunger strike. As media interest grew and journalists began to flock towards Marinaleda, other solidarity actions broke out elsewhere, many of them organised by the SOC, including a church occupation in nearby Morón de la Frontera, while 200 fellow *jornaleros* established four roadblocks on the Malaga-Seville trunk road.

'We will continue until they know there is hunger in Andalusia', read the *El País* headline on 17 August 1980, a quote from Sánchez Gordillo. It was a revealing line. The concrete demand for funds was only part of the battle: what was vital was that the rest of Spain, even the rest of the world, should be made aware of the region's plight.

A hunger strike was both a brave and canny choice. The normal repression meted out by the Guardia Civil and the government would not work this time. You can't arrest or beat someone for refusing food. Nothing could silence, in Sánchez Gordillo's words, 'the voice of hundreds of empty stomachs willing to continue, if necessary, until death'. The drama of the rhetoric reflected the desperation of the situation: Sánchez Gordillo spoke to the media in ominous tones, warning of outsiders who wished to make an example of Marinaleda, bourgeois *caciques* scared of these *comunistas*, people who dreamed of 'turning Marinaleda into Casas Viejas'. The invocation of that tragedy was knowingly provocative, but it was justified, too.

The hunger strike was launched in August, even though (or because) the heat would be at its most punishing, peaking above thirty-eight degrees every day. August, of course, is dead time for news, and the perfect opportunity to gain national media attention for systemic, ongoing stories like poverty via high-profile acts of vanguardist protest like this one. It allowed Sánchez Gordillo to proclaim to the world that they had received 'neither a telegram, nor a call, nor a promise' from the out-of-touch politicians busy sunning themselves on the beach; he added that 'the left too, are on vacation. They only come here for votes.' The heat made it more dangerous – doctors were on hand at all times, just in case – but also all the more remarkable, that men, women and children were going without food. Every day they would meet at the assembly to decide whether to continue, and to discuss the various messages of support they had received, as well as the attempts to reach those in power.

'We went out from the assembly very slowly,' wrote Sánchez Gordillo in a diary he kept of the hunger strike. 'Sweat has ravaged us. Some wring out their shirts – this is the sauna of the poor.'

The participation of the children of the village seems especially striking – they could see how desperate their parents' struggles for survival had become, and the total absence of work, and feel its effects on their households (and dinner plates). Going to bed hungry was a common occurrence. As one newspaper cartoon put it at the time: '700 on hunger strike in Marinaleda; the rest, just hungry.'

On day six of the strike, some of the children sat down and together wrote a letter to Prince Felipe, son of King Juan Carlos, heir to the throne, and, at the time, twelve years old. It was published in several Spanish newspapers. As far as the official record is concerned there was little adult involvement in the letter, and either way, it is a remarkable piece of propaganda:

The children of Marinaleda have the pleasure to tell you about the situation in Andalusia and specifically, Marinaleda. A few days ago, our parents, in an open assembly, agreed to go on hunger strike. We are in solidarity with them. We have been on hunger strike for several days.

Why are we on hunger strike? We are on hunger strike because our parents have already spent six months living on the alms of community employment. In our village people earn not even two hundred pesetas a day, because sometimes they only work two days a month. We live in such poverty that some families have to borrow money from their neighbours, because the shops no longer give them credit. Put yourself in our place and think: is it fair that while some children are on holiday with their parents and families, others don't know if they will eat that night? Is it fair that while some children have private tutors, others can't even attend state schools? Is it fair that while some waste large amounts of money on toys and luxuries, others have no shoes to wear and must go barefoot?

We don't think it is, and that is why we are on hunger strike. That is why we have gone several days without food, and we won't stop until a solution arrives, because this situation is unbearable. It is even more unbearable in a land as rich as Andalusia.

Friend: the problem in our land is serious, and so we are going to continue fighting alongside our parents. We will continue fighting because the problem is also ours; so please consider and answer these questions. What will become of us? Where is our future? Your future, we imagine, is already resolved, but what of ours? Who will resolve ours?

This is not a fairy tale, but a real situation which you will never know . . . We ask you with all our hearts to stop and think, and perhaps you'll feel anger or pity and you or your parents will give us some solution.

Sorry if these words are strong, but our hunger is stronger. Greetings from your friends. Marinaleda.

At the heart of this effort of undeniable collective energy, Mayor Sánchez Gordillo, still only thirty-one years old, was transforming into the person he would remain for decades. Notwithstanding his disapproval of leaders, he was more than a simple conduit for people power. Through his ineffable charisma he was leading the *pueblo*, as much as it was leading him. The people gathered for the general assembly were 'almost religious in their silence' when listening to Sánchez Gordillo, observed one visiting journalist – the only interruptions were outbursts of spontaneous applause. The assemblies closed with rousing shouts of '*¡Viva Andalucía!*' before Sánchez Gordillo implored everyone to go home and rest.

As the strike progressed, there were sympathy hunger strikes in neighbouring *pueblos* such as Osuna, Martín de la Jara, Aguadulce, Gilena and Los Corrales, as well as a general strike in Cabezas de San Juan. In Herrera, seven miles down the road, 200 workers locked themselves in the Chamber of Agriculture. As the days wore on, even more *pueblos* across Andalusia held assemblies to consider actions, occupations and demonstrations. The more desperate the situation got, the more its effects spiralled outwards – a truly successful expression of the anarchist tenet of 'propaganda of the deed'. Spain's minister of the interior returned from holiday; meetings were held, flimsy promises made, and still Marinaleda voted to continue the hunger strike.

The political tension rose with the medical danger to its participants. By the final full day of the strike, 22 August, people were regularly fainting, and suffering hypoglycaemia and crises of hypotension, while one man in his thirties was transferred to hospital in Seville.

At last, Labour Minister Salvador Sánchez Terán and Seville's civil governor, Isidro Pérez-Beneyto, effectively the leader of the region, returned from their holidays to address the crisis and, after numerous meetings, authorised a payment totalling 253 million pesetas for the Andalusian unemployed 'to last until the December olive harvest', as Marinaleda had demanded. While meeting the village's request, the politicians complained to the press that the whole thing had been exaggerated and cynically orchestrated for the benefit of the SOC union. They also claimed, somewhat implausibly, that the strike had had no effect on their decision to issue the emergency payment.

While the people of Marinaleda recovered, the unrest sparked by the hunger strike continued, with more hunger strikes elsewhere, *pueblo*-specific general strikes and occupations of government buildings – and solidarity demonstrations as far away as the Basque Country. Without the 253-million-peseta subsidy, it seems the hunger strike of 700 people in one small village could have spiralled into a full-blown regional uprising.

It was a Monday night in Palo Palo, back in December 2012, with León's country rock CDs playing softly in the background, harmonicas and long verses of longing delivered in Spanish. Monday nights are always very quiet in Andalusia – everyone has spent most of Sunday eating, drinking and socialising, and many restaurants and bars don't even open. There was a grand total of four of us in the bar: a businessman from Seville, delaying his journey home after visiting a friend, the landlord León, one other middle-aged local guy who often loiters around Palo, who called himself Michael, and me.

There was a Seville–Valladolid football game on TV, but it was going nowhere in particular, and the music was drowning out the commentary, so I got out my *Marinaleda – Huelga de Hambre Contra el Hambre* pamphlet, the more obscure of the two books written in 1980 that dealt with the hunger strike. After a while, Michael, equally bored by the game, noticed I was reading something in Spanish and asked if he could see it. With his leather jacket, slightly sad, gormless expression, and punky rat-tail haircut, he looked like the kind of guy who had arrived at middle age suddenly, due to a clerical error, and the surprise had devastated him.

'I've not seen this one before,' he muttered, turning it over in his hands. 'Man, that was a crazy year . . . We always have struggles here in Andalusia, but not usually like that. You know we were famous across the world? What a crazy summer.'

He flipped the pages slowly, spotting some familiar faces in the few photos at the back. He kept flicking through, and then his small sharp eyes zeroed in on one particular passage. He smiled, the only time I've ever seen him do so. 'I knew it!' He beckoned me to lean in. 'That's me! That interview is with me, Cornelio! That's my real name. I was only eleven.' He called León over from the bar. 'León, look – it's me!'

We read it together: he had been a strident young lad, resolute about joining the hunger strike and determined that the young people would remain as steadfast as their parents. 'Isn't this a lot to endure for an eleven-year-old?' the interviewer had asked him. 'We will endure it,' he replied. 'You haven't eaten anything?' 'Just water. We're going to carry on until they give us work. Or we'll have to emigrate.' Even at eleven he was ready to work, he told the incredulous interviewer – picking cotton, in a factory, anything.

Michael sighed. 'The situation is much better in Marinaleda now, of course,' he said. 'But we are still always fighting. Struggles, protests, demonstrations – here, in Seville, wherever.' I asked if Prince Felipe had ever answered their letter. He rolled his eyes slightly. 'What do you think?' he said, handed the book back to me, and turned back to the football.

In the mid-1990s, the Seville University anthropologist Félix Talego Vázquez lived in Marinaleda for a year, researching his doctoral thesis. This thesis was published as a controversial book – controversial in Marinaleda, anyway – whose title translates as *Worker Culture, People Power and Messianic Leadership*. Talego saw the relentless struggle of the early years as a vital part of the solidification of Sánchez Gordillo's leadership, not least during the hunger strike. Characterising your political project, as Sánchez Gordillo did, as *la voz de los sin voz* – the voice of those without a voice – and embarking on something as psychologically and emotionally significant as a group hunger strike, strengthens the distinction between an authentic, popular 'us' and a distant, oppressive, hegemonic 'them'. In view of Andalusia's history, I'm not sure this is an idea which requires much strengthening.

The hunger strike certainly went a long way in granting the man with the megaphone – both literally and figuratively, there is always one man holding Marinaleda's megaphone; he seems to carry the thing everywhere he goes – the right to speak for the *pueblo*. His older supporters in the village have told me that at a time when they had no voice, and had *never* had a voice throughout their history, they were happy that someone had a *megáfono*, and knew how to use it.

After centuries of being ignored, marginalised and near-starved, Marinaleda's skill at attracting the mass media was finally helping them address these problems. During the hunger strike, the village was inundated by the national press and TV along with the BBC, German TV, French, English, German and Catalan newspapers, and even *famosos*, celebrities like the Andalusian folk singer Carlos Cano. There was also an influx of leftist intellectuals, writers and politicians, clamouring to express their solidarity.

The strike was regarded as a success, wrote Talego, not because they acquired the funds to keep them going until the black olive harvest later that year, but because of the shockwaves they sent through the rest of Andalusia and Spain via the media: 'The press were to the Marinaleda hunger strike what the bride is to the wedding.' Sánchez Gordillo was certainly happy to see them, especially the foreign reporters from England and Germany: 'They gather a lot of material', he wrote in his hunger strike diary, 'to throw in the faces of those trying to lie. Thank goodness, because otherwise, the bourgeoisie had mounted a slander with enough clout to destroy and discredit the heroic struggle of the Andalusian *jornaleros*.'

It's no overstatement to say that the village itself was changed by the hunger strike. They were flattered by the attention, and perhaps even became fascinated by their own reflection. 'People were busy all morning reading the papers', wrote Talego, 'to find new stories in which they were the protagonists, to feel the almost magical thrill of seeing their friends and acquaintances displayed in pictures all through Andalusia and Spain.' Talego concluded that in this case at least, the observed object got pretty used to being observed, and rather enjoyed the experience.

From then on, reckons Talego, 'it was evident that Juan Manuel was someone special, different from the rest of those who were also on strike.' He's not wrong; Sánchez Gordillo proved then, and has been proving ever since, that he has a keen eye for the media. But why were the press interested? Why were their readers interested? Why did the coverage succeed, ultimately, in swaying a recalcitrant government? Perhaps because people wanted to hear what was coming from Sánchez Gordillo's megaphone.

Matters didn't stop there. In April 1981 there was another hunger strike over the continued lack of funds for community employment – futile work in any case, as Sánchez Gordillo said, which 'robs us of our dignity'.

This time, 315 workers went on hunger strike. In the first three months of 1981, the unemployed had only received funds to pay for two days of work per week, representing an income of 2,066 pesetas a week to support them and their families. It seems extraordinary now, but in that pre-internet world of communications, Marinaleda was so isolated that Pérez-Beneyto, the civil governor of Seville, thought he could get away with telling the newspapers that the hunger strike was not really happening. It would be a day or so before anyone would get there and be able to contradict him, which the newspapers duly did. What they reported did not make Pérez-Beneyto look any better.

'One day, all Andalusia will go up in flames,' one of Marinaleda's *jornaleros* told the press, contemplating the mud and weeds in the gutters he was clearing in exchange for his derisory community employment pay.

After a week on hunger strike, more cases of hypogly-caemia, fainting and malnutrition were reported by the doctors, and one old woman fell into a semi-comatose state. Hunger in Andalusia, said Sánchez Gordillo, is not merely 'a ghost running through the village. Hunger is a man of flesh and blood who has to support his children.' Four hundred people locked themselves into the village Sindicato building, where the assemblies happen now; the weaker ones lay on mattresses. In the town of Teba, also on hunger strike, a man died from complications relating to malnutrition. On this occasion, they secured a guarantee of four-days-per-week community employment for those without work.

But it was not enough. 'Return our stolen dignity!' demanded Sánchez Gordillo in a piece for *El País* in 1982, calling for 'real work', which could only come from redistribution of the land – not through community employment and stealing chickens.

'What is needed in Andalusia', he wrote, 'is a profound transformation of agricultural structures that generate wealth for a minority of landowners, and poverty, unemployment and hopelessness for the vast numbers of peasant labourers.'

And so they kept campaigning for changes to those agricultural structures, piece by piece. There were protests over the lack of water – for consumption, but also for irrigation – throughout the early 1980s. They were forced to share a well with the neighbouring towns of Gilena and El Rubio, and responded by occupying municipal buildings and scrawling *¡Queremos agua!* (We want water!) on their election ballots. For twenty-three days they staged a symbolic 'light strike', turning off all electric lights from 8 pm, a reference to the limited three or four hours they were allowed access to the well each day.

In fact, there was another well nearby, on the land of the Duke of Infantado. They tried to negotiate with him, hoping that El Rubio and Marinaleda could buy a certain amount of water every month. The Duke turned them down: he needed it to water his olive trees. The level of class hatred in this part of the world is difficult to grasp without these kinds of incidents in mind – it reads like a medieval struggle for basic sustenance, not Western Europe in the 1980s.

As Sánchez Gordillo and a few others locked themselves in the council building once again, the rest of the village voted for a hunger strike. After a few days of this, a solution was found (one suggested by Sánchez Gordillo at the start, but rejected by the regional government), with Marinaleda and El Rubio allowed into a consortium to run a pipe from a well in Écija. A few months later, a fresh supply was discovered in Estepa and a new well was dug there. Upon its official opening, Sánchez Gordillo addressed the soon-to-be mayor of Seville, Manuel del Valle Arévalo:

'We all know that soldiers fight, and generals just award themselves medals.'

'Yes,' del Valle replied, 'but you are a general, too.'

The people of Marinaleda fought on, winning one small victory at a time. But after several years they were still desperately poor, landless, and lacking in the autonomy they sought. They continued to involve themselves in every struggle going: farm and building occupations, strikes, lock-ins, marches, rallies. They went on hunger strike again over the arrest of fellow SOC *jornaleros* on demonstrations. They took another hunger strike to the Palacio de Monsalves in Seville, camping out outside the council of the Andalusian government, where some of their number proceeded to faint on the doorstep. Even what little work there was seemed under threat. In January 1983, seventy *marinaleña* women locked themselves in the village Sindicato in protest at the use of machinery in the olive harvest.

Their protests were creative, mobile, and often symbol-ically connected to the demands in question. In 1984 they occupied the Cordobilla reservoir for a month (eating, sleeping and holding assemblies there) to call for the crea-tion of a new dam which they said would irrigate 15,000 hectares of land in the Sierra Sur. Others occupied the

Cañada Honda hill near Gilena, to call for its reforestation with fruit-bearing trees.

They continued to incur the wrath of the political elites. When Prime Minister Felipe González, the supposedly socialist leader of the PSOE,** said in September 1983 that the farm labourers of Andalusia were using their community employment payments to buy cars, 600 *marinaleños* locked themselves in the Casa de Cultura in protest and began another hunger strike. The subsequent pattern followed a familiar path – silence from the politicians, followed by catcalls from Sánchez Gordillo via the press, escalation of the propaganda war, and finally establishment capitulation. González was embarrassed into atoning for his jibe by calling Sánchez Gordillo on the phone, to hear him out. And such was the media attention that when Sánchez Gordillo sent him a pilot plan for employment across Andalusia, González was compelled to announce he had read and considered it.

Sánchez Gordillo quickly became a media favourite; they described his 'almost messianic gestures', his trademark half-open shirt and prophet's beard, and were clearly impressed by his youth, his persistence and his unwavering ability to get up the noses of the authorities in new and newsworthy ways. He was 'perhaps the most charismatic character in the Andalusian countryside', one commentator wrote in 1983.

* * *

** *Partido Socialista Obrero Español*, Spanish Socialist Workers' Party.

In 1985, SOC labourers from Marinaleda and the nearby *pueblos* of Gilena and Utrera started to occupy the lands of the Duke of Infantado. He was four times over a *Grande de España*, a Spanish grandee, one of the most high-ranking members of the nobility, and owned 17,000 hectares in Andalusia. While the *jornaleros* engaged in cat-and-mouse occupations of the fields, chased off by the Guardia, Sánchez Gordillo was citing two feasibility studies which supported his recommendations for a dam of the Genil River that would allow the irrigation of 6,000 hectares and an expropriation of El Humoso's 1,200 hectares which would provide 250 families with jobs. Much was made of the oft-quoted statistic that 50 per cent of land in Andalusia was owned by 2 per cent of the families. Unemployment was 65 per cent in Marinaleda at the time.

'Why did you choose the Duke of Infantado's land specifically, and not someone else's?' my American friend Paulette asked Sánchez Gordillo when we met him in 2012. It's a fair question. If you're establishing micro-communism, there are bound to be imperfections in the levelling-out process, since by definition only a tiny part of the country is going to be communised; it seems a bit arbitrary. 'We chose his land because he was the one who had the most!' Sánchez Gordillo replied bluntly. There's something unscientific and pragmatic about this attitude which is quite refreshing.

The surviving Super-8 footage of the marches to occupy the Duke of Infantado's land now look so hallowed, so other-worldly. Sepia is already naturally the colour of the earth around Marinaleda, and the grainy, flickering images seem to plunge the period much further back into the past. The people of Marinaleda wound their way the ten miles from the village to El Humoso, in a stream four or five people wide and several hundred long. The most striking difference in the way they looked back then is that their shirts were plainer, in the prelapsarian simplicity of life before t-shirts with brands and pictures and symbols. Their white cotton clothes are yellowed by the old film, topped with olive or brown berets, the women in blue floaty dresses holding children and stirring great cauldrons of potato stew, wearing white headscarves against the scorching summer sun.

The flags they carried then were the Andalusian tricolour or an unadorned red flag. There is no Second Republic flag, and no custom-made utopia flag of Marinaleda yet: the badge of resistance was simply that of regional identity, or communism. Alongside the throng walks a younger, slimmer Sánchez Gordillo, his hair and beard black, still only in his early thirties, marshalling the marching column, rousing the troops with his megaphone, just as he does now. Back then, many were not confident of success – but in a sense they had little option but to persevere, and were continuously chivvied by the extraordinary persistence of the project and of its leader. 'I believe that over time', Sánchez Gordillo recalled recently, 'the small victories made people believe it was possible.'

Ever-present in that old footage are the cars of the Guardia Civil, who made sure to impede the villagers however they could. 'Arrested twice in 24 hours', read the front page of the now defunct *Diario 16* newspaper, under a photograph of a *marinaleña* in a headscarf, shielding her apparently shamed face from the camera. The regional government in Seville would keep sending orders for their eviction, but sometimes it took months to get the court orders – so the *marinaleños* stayed for months, eating and sleeping in makeshift shelters. They were not, in fact, disrupting anything much, in the sense that the land was not being used for anything at all – precisely their complaint. They were idle and the land was idle: the resolution was obvious. On this 1,200-hectare estate the only things growing, for miles in every direction, were wheat and sunflowers – it required only three or four caretakers to tend to it.

The Irish-Italian writer Michael Jacobs came across one of the farm occupations while researching his book *Andalusia*:

On the long drive up to the *cortijo* I passed a group of villagers carrying hoes and rakes, the women dressed in black. They could have been straight out of a communist poster of the 1930s and this impression was reinforced by the political badges they were all wearing. In the middle of all this prowled the leonine and instantly recognisable figure of Sánchez Gordillo, wearing a

Tolstoyan suit and a red sash. He addressed me in a slow solemn voice with no trace of a smile. I could not help feeling, confronted by such a manner and appearance, that I was in the presence of one of the Messianic figures who toured the Andalusian countryside in the nineteenth century.

It was land reform from below, not above, delivered by direct action, and always pacifist: their rule was to leave when evicted (though this did not prevent countless lawsuits for trespassing, roadblocks and other related incidents). They fell into a routine whereby the Guardia Civil would evict them every day at the same time, around 5 or 6 pm, when they would go peacefully and walk back to the village. The following morning they would walk the ten miles back again, flags held high. In the summer of 1985, in the blistering heat, they made the journey every day for a month – taking only Sunday off. Astonishingly, they even developed some cordial relationships with their lifelong enemies in the gendarmerie, such was the familiarity of the routine both sides fell into. Things were not always so smooth – some of the *marinaleños* were arrested and imprisoned (leading to more hunger strikes in sympathy), and in one incident in 1985, a shot was fired at an Andalusian flag flying above the heads of the occupiers: 'Fired by the same people who once did the same against Blas Infante, and with the same intention,' as Gordillo put it, displaying the shell casing for the photographers.

They carried out over 100 occupations of El Humoso during the 1980s, at one point camping in the property for ninety days and nights. As the 1992 Seville Universal Exposition approached, and the official rhetoric of civic excitement and pride intensified, Sánchez Gordillo was able to use his platform to contrast the hype ahead of the Expo with the ongoing deprivation in the Andalusian countryside, writing in 1989:

This human disaster occurs when all the official gran-diloquence teaches us 1992 will be the year that paradise begins – although it has not yet been clarified who for. 1992 is set before us as the new myth, in the hope we forget the ordeal we have been suffering. Indices of unemployment, emigration, illiteracy, and marginalisa-tion of all kinds are higher and sadder here than anywhere in Europe.

Taking the fight to Seville itself, they were blasted with water cannons away from the offices of the Expo commis-sioner general. In focusing on this high-profile, highly expensive vanity project, with millions already spent and millions of tourists expected, they had finally broken the Andalusian government. After months of negotiations behind closed doors, in 1991 they were finally granted El Humoso's 1,200 hectares, the Duke of Infantado was quietly paid off by the regional government, the Junta de Andalucía, and the people of Marinaleda finally became

landlords. The Duke didn't even put up much of a fight in the end, Sánchez Gordillo told me – he got compensation from the government and had barely even been using the land, which in any case was a tiny proportion of all that he owned. 'Honestly, I think we did the Duke a favour,' Sánchez Gordillo said, straight-faced.

It was a historic victory. In Sánchez Gordillo's reading – and he had once been a part-time history teacher in Marinaleda – it was the first time in 5,000 years that the Andalusian farm labourers had been given the land that was rightfully theirs.

They didn't rest on their laurels, but continued *la lucha* throughout the 1990s, campaigning for funds for cultural projects, for housing, or for their brethren across Andalusia: occupying the Bank of Spain, blocking the high-speed AVE trains, breaking into the international airports at Malaga and Seville, occupying the Palace of San Telmo, Canal Sur Radio, and launching yet more hunger strikes, demonstrations and blockades, in the Sierra Sur and in Seville.

It's not been without consequences: during the 1980s campaign for land, especially, there were constant arrests, beatings and trials. Even now, every time I visit Marinaleda, Sánchez Gordillo seems to be either facing court or just having left it, on charges relating to some protest or other – normally he only gets a fine. Was it true, I asked him in 2012, that he'd been in jail seven times and had fascist agitators try to kill him not once, but twice?

'Yes, that's right,' he said, with a hint of a smile. You're nobody if you haven't survived an assassination attempt or two, right? 'The first time was in the 1980s, at the beginning of our struggle. A man from Fuerza Nueva, an extreme-right party, sort of like Le Pen's, shot at me. I was in the car, and the bullet went in one door and out the other.' He mimed a bullet whizzing past him, eyes wide. 'The other attempt happened when ETA killed a [Partido Popular] councillor in the Basque Country called Miguel Ángel Blanco. The same day one of the Guardia Civil said that since one of their side had been killed, they should shoot someone from the left. One of them came to my house with a gun, but I saw him in time and had him stopped.' Sánchez Gordillo seemed calmly stoical about his own punishments. When you have thought about – and fought – power for as long as he has, you become almost zen about it.

'I have been in jail many, many times and I have been harassed numerous times more. I believe in non-violence, and the community uses non-violent means to fight. Power uses violence when something of theirs is touched that they don't want touched. The bourgeoisie is pro-democracy only as long as democracy doesn't hurt their pockets.' And if it does? 'If it does, they stop being democratic: they send the police, they start a war, they stage a coup. They have no scruples. Yes, they speak of peace. They speak of peace, but practise war.'

※   ※   ※

Back in the olive oil factory, Bigotes refused to lend his whiskers to any kind of complacency about Marinaleda's remarkable achievements. And yet for him everything changed after 1991, when they won the land which stretched out before us:

'We've now reached a level where utopia is a different idea. When we started, we were starving. We've been fighting for a long time, we've got the prizes we struggled for in Marinaleda: we have work, we have all these facilities, everything is cool now. We won. Now we are protesting to solve the crisis, which is a global problem.'

He gestured towards the fields, and the hills of Estepa beyond. The mist rolled off the top of the olive groves of El Humoso, sweeping down over the Duchess of Alba's land, south towards Marinaleda and El Rubio.

'We're fighting for another kind of utopia now: the future. The future is going to be very interesting.'

4

The Land Belongs to Those Who Work It

For a part of the world which spends most of its life immersed in bright sunlight, Marinaleda is remarkably active in the dark: before the sun rises, and after sunset – not least in the devastating heat of the summer, when temperatures can reach forty-nine degrees, as they did in August 2012. You try and sweep the dust off your patio, one *marinaleña* told me, and find yourself dripping sweat straight onto the floor you're supposed to be cleaning. It was scarcely worth doing anything before the sun went down, when temperatures declined to a more reasonable thirty-five degrees or so. It also made work of all kinds nearly impossible; but the Andalusians are used to it, and carry on regardless, slowly, with cold drinks and sun hats.

In the darkness of a winter morning, between 6 and 7 am, Marinaleda's workers are clustered around the counter of the orange-painted patisserie, Horno el Cedazo. Here they stand, knocking back strong, dark coffee accompanied by orange juice, pastries and *pan con tomate*: truly one of the world's best breakfasts, a large hunk of toast served alongside a bottle of olive oil and a decanter of sweet, salty, pink tomato pulp. Pour on one, then the other, then a sprinkling of salt and pepper, and you are ready for a day in the fields. Those with stronger stomachs also knock back a shot of one of the lurid-coloured liquors arrayed on a high shelf behind the counter; the syrupy, pungent anís is the most popular of these coffee chasers.

Tucked away in a corner of the bakery is a stand selling lottery tickets – phenomenally popular across Spain – with millionaire prizes called things like *El Joker*. The big advertisement behind the lottery desk is for EuroMillones, a colossal mega-lottery that runs across Europe, with a minimum prize of €15 million: the poster features a brown brick wall cut away to reveal a glimpse of a tropical paradise, clear blue seas, and a yacht sailing off into the sunset. The slogan, written in mock graffiti on top of the brickwork, says '*LA LIBERTAD ES EL PREMIO*'. Freedom is the prize. The troika, you feel, would approve of this kind of utopian dreaming, this consumerist vision of freedom.

All work in the Marinaleda co-operative is shift work, depending on what needs harvesting, and how much of it there is. If there's enough work for your group, then you will be told in advance, through the loudspeaker on the van that circles the village the previous evening. It's a strange, quasi-Soviet experience, sitting at home and hearing the van drive past announcing 'Work in the fields tomorrow for Group B'. The static-muffled announcements get louder and quieter as the van winds through the village's narrow streets, like someone lost in a maze carrying a transistor radio.

If you don't have your own car to drive to El Humoso for work, then you get a lift: mutual aid and co-operation underscores a great deal of the town's farming work, in practice as well as principle. Visiting the farm with a photographer friend during the annual olive harvest, without benefit of wheels, we were passed from favour to favour all day in a chain of instinctive, unthinking acts of kindness. We had been invited to a mid-morning breakfast at 10 am by Manolo, the *jefe* (boss) of the olive oil factory, and were struggling a bit trying to work out how to get there. In the 1980s, the *marinaleño* occupiers had walked those ten miles along the road every single morning in the summer heat; we, however, were rather hoping for a lift. But all of my friends in the village were busy or working elsewhere, and the people actually working in the fields had all set off at the crack of dawn.

Eventually, after ringing around a bit, we were told: 'Turn up at this address on Avenida de la Libertad and ring the doorbell, a guy called Pepe will take you.' I'd never met Pepe before, but he was quite happy to give up half his morning to drive us out to the farm; he was a history buff, and delighted in telling us about the old days – he even showed us his blog before we set off. Once we arrived at the oil factory at the entrance to El Humoso it quickly became clear that Pepe knew Manolo, and José, and Bigotes

– they're all the same generation, all fifty-plus, all guys who were in the village since the project began; so Pepe joined us for breakfast, too.

In some kind of teleological mistake, we started at the end, not with hours of hard physical labour, but with the epic breakfast which ought to be its reward. In a small rec room off the main factory floor, on a shiny plastic table-cloth, were laid pieces of kitchen towel, and a single rugby-ball-shaped loaf of bread for each of us – the kind with orange-coloured crusts that are so hard they could probably be hurled, quarterback-style, across a factory floor and still remain intact. We were shown what to do next. You cut the loaf lengthways to create two giant half-moons of bread, then push your thumbs into the fluffy white dough to make some space, before taking the unmarked jug of olive oil and pouring its rich green contents into the cavity, so it seeps into the dough. You then devour these giant half moons of fruity olive oil bread with pieces of *jamón* from the leg clamped to its special stand, slices of manchego cheese, and chunks of peppery *salchichón*, hacked off and eaten in lumps. The oil was fresh out of the vats, yet to be bottled, and actually tasted of the aromatic air you smell deep in the olive groves.

'Would you like a drink? Some coffee?' offered Manolo. 'Or wine?' We laughed, and opted for coffee. It hadn't been a joke. Manolo's brother José, who manages the land, and whose overalls suggested he had done more that morn-ing than I had all week, opted for wine. Manolo reached up to a box of white wine on a shelf behind the coffee machine, and held down the little tap until he had filled a decent-sized tumbler of the stuff.

When we finished we gathered around the *Huelga de Hambre* pamphlet, and their faces lit up with that same mixture of slight bemusement, joy and poignancy I'd seen before in veterans of *la lucha*. They flicked to the pictures and started spotting old friends in among the wide-angle shots of various historic general assemblies and marches. It was a tad macabre. 'He's dead,' said Manolo, as if commentating on a football match. 'She's dead, too.' You remember all these events, I asked, even though it was thirty-three years ago? 'Sure, of course. I was at that meeting, it went on for hours.' He breathed deeply and handed the book over to his brother. 'You must understand the connection', he insisted, 'between all that' – he pointed to the yellowing pamphlet – 'and all this. Everything here', he said, casting his arm out at the factory around him, 'comes from the struggle.'

Manolo went on to tell me disdainfully about another book, a stupid book by someone who did not understand all this history, who did not understand the suffering and deprivation of the old days. It was, of course, the Félix Talego book. Talego is an anthropologist, not a right-wing critic out to destroy the village, but since the title of the book included the phrase 'messianic leadership', it's not hard to see why the members of the co-operative, supporters of Sánchez Gordillo, took against him. I feigned

ignorance of Talego, not wanting to associate myself with
another suspicious outsider who asked a lot of questions
– and chose the wrong answers.

As breakfast was tidied away, my photographer friend
Dave showed them some of the photos he'd taken of the
olive oil factory, flicking the wheel around on the back of
his digital camera. As he reached the end of the selection of
pictures of El Humoso, he accidentally flicked onto some
portraits he had taken the previous day of Mariano Pradas,
the village's PSOE leader and long-standing enemy of
Sánchez Gordillo, which he hadn't got around to deleting
from the memory card. There was a sharp intake of breath
from the workmen. 'Oh,' said Manolo. 'The opposition.'
And made a face.

The solidarity of struggle binds people together in an
almost ineffable way through a shared experience, a shared
goal, shared risks and hardships. 'Solidarity', when practised over decades by one community fighting a distant,
hated other, becomes a psychological state. Combine this
with the comradeship of working together every day, on a
project which is the spoils of your struggle, and you have a
kind of loyalty greater even than the sum of those two
parts. You feel it in the way the older *marinaleños* talk about
the old days in general, but it comes across even more
powerfully from that generation when they talk about *el
alcalde*, the mayor, and his enemies: these guys were with
Sánchez Gordillo since the beginning.

*   *   *

As soon as the 1,200-hectare farm was won in 1991, cultivation began. The new Marinaleda co-operative selected crops that would need the greatest amount of human labour, to create as much work as possible. In addition to the ubiquitous olives and the oil processing factory, they planted peppers of various kinds, artichokes, fava beans, green beans, broccoli: crops that could be processed, canned, and jarred, to justify the creation of a processing factory which provided a secondary industry back in the village, and thus more employment. 'Our aim was not to create profit, but jobs,' Sánchez Gordillo explained to me. This philosophy runs directly counter to the late-capitalist emphasis on 'efficiency' – a word which has been elevated to almost holy status in the neoliberal lexicon, but in reality has become a shameful euphemism for the sacrifice of human dignity at the altar of share prices.

Sánchez Gordillo once suggested to me that the House of Alba could invest their vast riches (from shares in banks and power companies, as well as multi-million-euro agricultural subsidies for their vast tracts of land) to create jobs, but they've never shown any interest in doing so. 'We believe the land should belong to the community that works it, and not in the dead hands of the nobility.' That's why the *latifundio* owners plant wheat, he explained – wheat can be harvested with a machine, overseen by a few caretakers; in Marinaleda, crops like artichokes and tomatoes are chosen precisely because they need lots of labour. Why, the logic runs, should 'efficiency' be the most important value in society, to the detriment of human life?

The town co-operative does not distribute profits: any surplus is reinvested to create more jobs. Everyone in the co-op earns the same salary, forty-seven euros a day for six and a half hours of work: it may not sound like a lot, but it's more than double the Spanish minimum wage. *Jornalero* participation in decisions about what crops to farm, and when, is encouraged, and often forms the focus of the village's general assemblies – in this respect, being a *cooperativista* means being an important part of the functioning of the *pueblo* as a whole. Where once the day labourers of Andalusia were politically and socially marginalised by their lack of an economic stake in their *pueblo*, they are now – at least in Marinaleda – called upon to lead the way. Non-co-operativists are by no means excluded from involvement in the town's political, social and cultural life – it's more that if you *are* a part of the co-operative, you can't really avoid being swept up in local activities, outside the confines of the working day.

Many visitors to Marinaleda seem to expect the rhetoric about autonomy and self-sustainability to mean that everything grown on the land is consumed in the village, with nothing imported or exported. It doesn't quite work like that: they'd have an unusually pimento-heavy diet if they operated according to the principles of subsistence farming in Marinaleda. The produce is certainly sold in the village: you can find the El Humoso logo on jars and tins of vegetables in the few grocery shops, including the Basque-owned supermarket Eroski, the closest Marinaleda has to a 'big name' chain store, the size of a small 7-Eleven one might find in a major city. The other 'supermarket' is Coviran, also a grocery chain, and about the same size as most *marinaleños'* living rooms. But the bulk of El Humoso produce is sold outside the village, all over Spain and even abroad.

It would be churlish to reproach them for it, but inevitably, the unique context for the co-operative's produce is made very clear in its marketing: 'Know that when you consume any product from our co-operative, you are helping to create employment and social justice'. Why not, suggests the website, show your support for this 'alternative solidary economy'? Sánchez Gordillo found himself making a similar case in 2012, when he spent two and a half weeks visiting Venezuela, doing numerous TV interviews and speeches: he eventually persuaded Chávez's lieutenants to invest state money in buying olive oil from the co-operative – a big deal for the village, in every sense.

After our breakfast in the olive oil factory, Dave and I asked if we could see the olive harvest in action, since we had come at the right time of year. Sure, Manolo said. It was another glorious sunny winter day, and I asked if we could walk it. He laughed and shook his head. '1,200 hectares is a lot, you know?' The harvest was happening far away, far too far; literally miles away from the farm

buildings and the road, over the rolling hills, beyond the
TIERRA UTOPIA mural, beyond the horizon.

So we were passed along a series of men in green overalls, piled into a mud-splattered 4x4 with Antonio and set
off along the bumpy, soggy paths through the fields. Somewhere along the way our back wheel sunk deep into a
muddy hole and we ground to a halt: the wheel spun and
spun, but there was nothing doing. While Antonio went
off to look for help, we stood amid the endless symmetrical
rows of twelve-foot olive trees. It was like being lost in a
forest, but with no canopy overhead blocking out the light,
just blue sky. It took him about half an hour to reappear,
accompanied by a tractor to tow us out. At one point we
spotted another group of pickers, about a quarter of a mile
from the path, bent low over the reddish-brown pepper
plants in the distance.

When we arrived at the harvest site we found about
forty people taking in the olives, sweating away in grubby
t-shirts and roughed-up jeans. Spain not only cultivates
more olives than any other country on earth, it cultivates
more than the second, third, fourth and fifth countries in
the list (Italy, Greece, Morocco and Turkey) put together.
Marinaleda's olive oil is described as hand-crafted, which it
mostly is, but they do get some help from a wonderful
piece of machinery: the tree shaker. This bit of kit grasps
the tree trunk about a third of the way down with
outstretched metal arms, like Homer Simpson grabbing
Bart's neck. The driver then presses 'shake', and it proceeds

to throttle the tree frenetically, while the olives rain down in their hundreds – aided by two men with ten-foot aluminium poles whose job it is to whack the branches while it's shaking. It's basic physics, but it works.

After about thirty seconds of this, when the downpour of fresh olives has been reduced to a trickle, the machine releases the tree, reverses away, and swings around to attack the next. Meanwhile, the workers move in for the exhausting next phase. They gather up the vast nets that now contain hundreds, perhaps thousands of olives, tie the nets at the corners, and, with the bunched end held with both hands over one shoulder, lean into the hard slog of dragging the nets through the rows of trees to where the truck is waiting to take them back for processing. The men and women are inclined at the same narrow angle to the ground as the guys who pull articulated lorries in World's Strongest Man competitions. They looked about as determined, so we tried not to get in their way.

As late morning turned into early afternoon, another smiling chap in green overalls offered us a lift back to the farmhouse where we had begun, and we decided to take it – we didn't want to get stuck out there. This time, it transpired, we would be travelling in a rather more old-school way: in the back of an olive truck, clinging onto the sides, supported by the rustic cushion of thousands of freshly harvested olives. 'Have you tried squeezing them between your fingers?' asked Dave. I squeezed, and managed to hit myself right in the eye with the gloriously fragrant gloop of fresh olive oil. It smelt amazing on my fingertips, toasting in the December sunshine: some consolation for the temporary blindness.

At the farmhouse we hung around some more, taking photos and idly wondering how to get home, when another white 4×4 pulled up, and a big, rectangular wardrobe of a man in his fifties leaned out and asked if we needed to get back to the village. His name escapes me now, but it's fairly safe to assume he was called Antonio. It was getting near lunchtime – Spanish lunchtime; English lunchtime had long since passed – and so the traffic was going in the right direction. The working day in the fields is over by 3 pm.

So we chuntered along the blessedly flat roads, back towards Marinaleda, with Estepa looming halfway up the hill in the distance to the right. Are these lands part of El Humoso too? I asked, gesturing at the olive rows around us. No, these are all fairly small holdings, private lands, he explained, mostly owned by people from the neighbouring *pueblo* of El Rubio, the kind of farms run by one family, perhaps with a little help from hired labourers at harvest time. We've visited El Rubio, I told him: in a way, it's not really so different from Marinaleda, right? Another small Andalusian *pueblo* with lots of *jornaleros*, some tapas bars, and a carnival?

He briefly turned his head away from the road ahead and looked at me like I was a small child. 'It's completely different.' That told me.

*   *   *

The land – the dirt, the earth itself – is not only deemed to be a sovereign right, a home; in a deep sense, it is almost part of the *jornalero*'s DNA. *La tierra* is exalted throughout Sánchez Gordillo's rhetoric, and in the language of his political fellow travellers, the SOC-SAT and men like Diego Cañamero. This is both geographical and historical: to be surrounded by it and denied ownership of it, for so long, gives the earth a very different hue. But this unwavering focus on the land as the ultimate goal leaves no room for diversification or distraction: there is never a suggestion, or even a consideration, that utopia might be protected and furthered by the expansion of job creation into other areas. Marinaleda's motto – one of its many mottos – is 'Land to the tiller'. That is what they as a *pueblo* are destined to do.

It's a philosophy which positions 1991 as their teleological end-point; this is their End of History.

Some of the British ex-pats living in the village suggested to me that, given the crisis, now was the time for the Ayuntamiento to capitalise on Marinaleda's increasing fame and create some kind of gift shop, selling t-shirts and baseball caps and all the usual tat, emblazoned with the village name and crest. They're certainly right that there are enough visitors to sustain such an enterprise; there always have been, but especially since the actions and expropriations of August 2012. Tourists and travellers flock from Spain and Europe just for the night to see this notorious little village for themselves, while others come in from Seville, Malaga or Valencia for concerts at Palo Palo. Just imagine, Len laughed, you could buy a combination costume of a Palestinian keffiyeh, a checked shirt and a straw hat, to look like the mayor, and a mouse mat with *una utopia hacia la paz* on it. León at Palo Palo sells t-shirts, after all. 'He's got some sense. But the mayor will never do it. He's only interested in the land. But it's stupid! They don't have work – and people would buy that crap, of course they would.'

Private enterprise as such is permitted in the village – not only legally, but perhaps more importantly, it is *permitted*, an accepted part of life. As with the seven privately owned bars and cafés in the village (the Sindicato bar is owned by the union), if you wanted to open a pizzeria or a little family business of any kind, no one would stand in your way. But if a hypothetical Head of Regional Development and Franchising for, say, Carrefour, or Starbucks, with a vicious sense of humour and a masochistic streak, decided this small village was the perfect spot to expand operations, well – they wouldn't get very far. 'We just wouldn't allow it,' Sánchez Gordillo told me bluntly.

The point is that Marinaleda is not, in the full extent of its economic operations, a communist village. Or at the very least, in the Soviet analogy, it's more NEP than War Communism, a mixed economy that permits the generation of some small-scale private profit, rather than an all-encompassing, centrally planned control economy.

There are a number of privately owned farms, mostly small plots of land owned by a single family, enough to sustain an extended family in work and income, but not enough to provoke the ire of the *cooperativistas*, or Sánchez Gordillo. Even in the case of the few families with enough work to sporadically employ others, usually to help with harvests, there is an obvious – and widely recognised – distinction between that kind of land ownership and the *latifundios* owned by the Houses of Alba and Infantado. No one in this part of the world seems to be absolutist about property and profit, and consequently the kulaks aren't nervously looking over their shoulders.

In 2013, the subjectivity of the *marinaleño* worker is self-consciously different to that in the world outside. Left or right, no one is ignorant of this exceptionalism, based on the fact that El Humoso works towards a common goal, for the benefit of a collective, not an individual, and that it is part of something bigger than the farm itself. And yet, in a day-to-day sense, the attitude to work itself is much the same as anywhere else. 'It's really tiring, it's hard work,' is the first response of most young – and not so young – *marinaleños* to questions about work in the fields. 'It's boring and repetitive' is the most common description of work on the factory production line. Neither of these assessments is exactly surprising. A change in socio-political context or labour organisation, however dramatic, does little to change the nature of work itself.

But not a single *marinaleño* I met neglected to mention the socio-political context of that work, the history of the struggle to create it, or the parlous situation in the rest of crisis-hit Spain. The lament about work being boring, tiring or unstimulating was always followed by a 'but': but at least we have it *here*. But at least we have it *now*. But at least we have it *together*. But at least we fought and won it *for ourselves*.

With an average of 36 per cent unemployment across Andalusia in 2013, soaring above 50 per cent in some towns, and a history of 65 per cent unemployment in Marinaleda in the 1980s, no one is ignorant of how bad it was, and how bad it could be. The *marinaleño* attitude to work is best explained not as 'striving for the sake of striving', as if there was something innately noble about work, but as striving for autonomy – for the dignity that comes from people's sovereignty over their own survival.

Autonomy is at the core of the local philosophy: the elevation of individual freedom intrinsic to the nineteenth-century anarchism which blew like wildfire through this region. 'In this community', wrote a visiting journalist during the 1980 hunger strike, 'the concepts of work and autonomy are unified.' *Jornaleros*, as farm-workers without land, could never be said to be truly free without a sovereignty over their work, and the basic stability of not having to migrate hundreds of miles from home in order to get it.

Without this context in mind, the Marinaleda attitude can appear to outsiders as a kind of miniature

Stakhanovism: there are constant demands for the right to work, accentuating the sense that you can only prove your political fidelity (to the struggle, to the collective, above all to the *pueblo*) through work.

When Spanish social security took the form of 'community employment' in the early 1980s, the people of Marinaleda responded by campaigning for land, and for work, rather than the humiliation of doing 'government jobs' not dissimilar to those prescribed as sentences by the judiciary. The only visible difference between community employment and a chain gang, in fact, was the lack of physical chains. Throughout the 1980s, the unemployed *jornaleros* of the south were accused, as poor communities so often are, of fecklessness and even fraud – normally by politicians from the north. In the first of many media-savvy stunts, Marinaleda responded by working harder for free, as this *El País* report from March 1981 records:

> Unemployed agricultural workers of the Seville town of Marinaleda unanimously decided to expand their work day in community employment to seven hours a day, instead of the six hours officially stipulated, as a show of real will to work, and to protest allegations of fraud and *picaresca* [rogueish behaviour].

In 1982, when the community employment fund was temporarily withdrawn and several Andalusian towns went on strike, Marinaleda voted in its assembly to continue working, even without pay. In August that year, Sánchez Gordillo addressed a rally of 8,000 farm labourers in Seville, saying that what was needed was real work, not charity: 'If they still do not understand, from this event, that we want to work the land, well: we will have to act differently.'

One of the most well-known symbolic and practical activities of Marinaleda is the ritual of *Domingos Rojos*, Red Sundays. Once a month – so the theory goes – the people of the village gather on a Sunday morning outside the Sindicato, usually as early as 8 am, and, depending on individual capabilities, and a popular vote on what needs doing most urgently, the participants proceed to spend the day working voluntarily to improve the village. This could mean gardening in the public park, painting murals, sweeping the streets, or helping bring in the harvest in El Humoso.

Red Sundays were born out of an argument between the *pueblo* and Prime Minister Felipe González. In a 1983 speech González (an Andalusian himself) dusted off the old canard that Andalusian farm labourers were lazy and accused them of spending their community employment pay on luxuries like cars. Marinaleda held a Saturday night assembly and decided to devote the next day to improving the *pueblo*. Sánchez Gordillo called up the press and informed them as follows:

'We want to demonstrate that in order to find laziness and corruption, the prime minister should look not at the Andalusian *jornaleros*, but somewhere closer to home. We want to show him that when the government rests, the *jornaleros* are working.'

And so the next day, they set about several hours of street repair, painting and landscaping in the public squares. It was a defiant performance to the outside world, and a humiliation for the prime minister.

Beyond their propaganda role, Talego's observation on Red Sundays was that they also played a big part in solidifying community sensibility and tightening the bonds of the *pueblo* – thus boosting participation and faith in *the project*. This was, Talego suggested, a two-way street: when dishing out paid work at El Humoso, it would be relevant whether you had participated in Red Sundays – just like individuals' participation in demonstrations, general assemblies and even village festivities would be informally, unofficially noticed.

More than that, though, voluntary work arguably changes the labour relation. Marinaleda exists in a capitalist world, but proving that 'we can work for reasons other than money' is, for Sánchez Gordillo, an act of subversion of capitalism in itself. It is one situated in the history of some of the mayor's idols – heroes of the Cuban revolution like Che, and even some Soviet figures.

The primacy of work and land within the Marinaleda mythology comes less easily to the younger generation, who did not spend their formative years denied it, nor struggled throughout their lives to get it. Moreover, modern technology and transportation has dissolved the hard boundaries of the *pueblo* – and its tight occupational possibilities – in a way that would have been inconceivable 100 or even thirty years ago. The Andalusian *jornalero* identity – with its unique iteration in each *pueblo* – has been remarkably tenacious over the centuries, but the fact is that both culture and people now seep in and out of the borders of each town with incredible ease. Cheap cars, cheap flights and the internet have flattened the landscape.

'A thousand euros a month is fine – 1,200 a month is pretty good,' Cristina, a young law graduate, told me one evening as we nursed our *cañitas* of cheap lager. We were talking about the *mileuristas*, her generation, so christened because they had learned to get by on one thousand euros (*mil euros*) per month. The Spanish minimum wage works out at €600– 700 a month, and unemployment benefit is generally €500–600 per month. Cristina was living with her mother in Marinaleda while also renting a room in a flat in Estepa, where she works as a teacher some of the week. She lives a dual life, she explained: she loves her life in the larger *pueblo*, shared with other people her age; it offered an escape of sorts from an unfortunately prolonged adolescence. Her peers in Estepa tell the same story – many of them are thirty or above and still live with their parents.

Cristina's parents are *marinaleños*, and moved to Barcelona in the great exodus of the 1960s, when there was no work in the fields. Like so many, they returned in the 1980s because the situation had changed. Despite the long absence, they were always, of course, sons and daughters of the *pueblo*. Cristina was schooled in the new post-Franco Catalan education system, and almost everyone in her class was a Spanish emigrant – there were people from Extremadura, Galicia, Andalusia, and only about four or five Catalans. 'It gave me a big belief in cosmopolitanism,' she told me. 'People were sharing their cultures from across Spain. One child would say, "at home we eat this kind of food", another would say, "ah, well, my mother cooks the stew like this . . ."'

In the perfect storm of Ryanair, *la crisis*, and the internet, a new kind of wanderlust-by-necessity is detectable among Spain's younger generations – and it has infiltrated Marinaleda, too. There is a growing sense that the current Spanish *juventud sin futuro*, youth without a future, will only find one by emigrating. Cristina had this same *zeitgeist* mixture of despair – she's been unemployed before – and sense of adventure and excitement when she considers that leaving the country might be her only option. I'd love to see London, she said, agonising, as she often did, about the quality of her English skills – she badly needed to pass her imminent English exams, she felt, in order to get out.

In 2013, everyone knows that full employment in Marinaleda is a myth. In fact, it's not even fair to call it a myth: 'They don't *really* have full employment!' is a straw man set up by right-wing critics of the village. Sánchez Gordillo's line in interviews in recent years has been: 'We have almost full employment.' This is correct, according to the official statistics from the Junta de Andalucía: the unemployment rate in the village is 5 to 6 per cent.

The situation is certainly tougher now than it has been for a long time. One evening in the Centro de Adultos, where evening classes take place, I picked up a Youth of Marinaleda Bulletin, a monthly four-page leaflet produced by the town hall. Alongside notices of go-karting and basketball tournaments, and courses in 'personal marketing' for budding entrepreneurs, laid on by the Andalusian Youth Institute, was a page of jobseeker websites including summerjobs.com, pickingjobs.com, holidayresortjobs.com, workingholidayguru.com, gapwork.com. Almost all of them offered short-term, seasonal work orientated around harvests and holiday high seasons on the coast. On the back was another page devoted to job vacancies, advertising work in McDonald's, Toys R Us and Disneyland – or, for anyone willing to travel not just beyond the *pueblo*, but beyond the Spanish border, there was the possibility of cleaning jobs in France.

In a sense, it was ever thus. The modish idea of 'the precariat' describes the group experiencing ever-worsening labour conditions under late capitalism following the slow disintegration of the job-for-life, with its relatively stable, union-backed working conditions and pensions. In Spain this is a process which Prime Minister Rajoy's landmark, detested labour reforms of 2011 have deliberately accelerated (for the good of the economy, naturally). But for Andalusian *jornaleros*, short-term contracts, long periods without work, permanent financial insecurity and poverty pay have been the norm for centuries. In a region which never really experienced Fordism – the standardised system of industrial mass production embodied by the Ford Motor Company in the United States – post-Fordism is a slightly meaningless concept. For young *marinaleños* who can't, or don't want to, work as a *cooperativista* in El Humoso, these less than tantalising job offers are just a continuation of the labour conditions of their ancestors before 1979 – neo-feudalism with a Disney smile.

In Somonte, the latest, most high-profile piece of Andalusian anarchist land expropriation, I had seen a sophisticated mural which expressed a sentiment I had expected to hear more of in the crisis. Painted in green on the side of a white farmhouse building, in large capitals, it read *Andalusians – don't emigrate, fight!* Further down, underneath stencilled portraits of Zapata, Malcolm X, Geronimo and Blas Infante, was a quote from the latter: *The land is yours: reclaim it!*

I've encountered almost no resentment of the people emigrating in search of work – but then the generation of *ninis* (neither work nor study) are not the first to face this dilemma: their parents had to do the same, and their parents before that. The only difference is now you emigrate on a cheap flight to Berlin or London, rather than hitching a slow ride to the fields or factories of the north.

Despite the lack of reproach, those leaving certainly felt guilt and sadness. I recall one Spanish friend speaking to me very quickly in English about his plans to leave, for the third time in five years, to go and work in Berlin (following Stockholm and London). He had to speak fast because his mother, who didn't understand much English, was in the living room with us watching television, and he hadn't yet mustered the courage to tell her he was leaving again.

Outside Marinaleda, the situation for other young Andalusians is devastating. Once, at a bar in Estepa, a young man called Jesús joined us. I asked him the same broad questions I asked everyone, about the economy, about the government, about the future. He clasped his face with one cradling hand – he was weary but stoical, like a cargo ship buffeted by strong winds. 'Things are getting worse everywhere. Wages are now even lower, and contracts are shorter. If you have graduated from university, you must go to Germany or America or England to get a job.' Spain has the highest proportion of graduates of any country in Europe – for all the good it is doing them now. There were two options, Jesús said. Either live with your parents, spend all your time looking for work, go out and protest occasionally, or join the hordes scuttling down the brain-drain to points beyond Spain.

What about Marinaleda, as an alternative? He shrugged. It's good that you can have a free house and a job there, but it's not all great, he said. 'You know you have to work on Sundays?'

In Seville, a woman in her mid-twenties called Emma told me that about 90 per cent of her friends were out of work, and most of them had had to move back into their family homes after a few fleeting years of adult freedom. 'I'm talking about all different kinds of people, people with no qualifications, people who have a masters, people who have two degrees.' She went on:

'It's really, *really* bad here. Seville had so many building companies before the "brick crisis", as we call it. You have so many unemployed young and not so young people with no other qualification than to work in construction. We have thousands of flats where construction just stopped, and the buildings are left half-finished.' These relics of late capitalism scar the whole Spanish landscape now.

A lot of her friends left school when they were fifteen, Emma explained. The authorities didn't really mind, because they knew there was work available, and they needed people to do it. 'The government just said, "Okay, leave school, go!" So now in the south you have a lot of young unemployed people with no qualifications, but they have a house and they have a family and they have a loan, and they need to pay for everything – and they can't go back to school, because they have responsibilities. What are you going to do in that situation?'

There is little else to do but come out into the plazas, in fact – either to idle, or to organise. Access to the monthly unemployment benefit is being limited, she said, with new applicants blocked by bureaucracy – because the government's austerity programme simply can't afford to give it to everyone who is unemployed; there are just too many of them.

Back in Marinaleda we were invited to visit one of the *casitas*, the self-built houses, belonging to a family with two grown-up children facing up to the realities of the crisis-era job market. The invite had come via Javi's twenty-seven-year-old friend Ezequiel, who I'd met once in London, when he was a diffident young man lost in the big city, mute from lack of English, slightly perplexed at my enthusiasm for his obscure little *pueblo*. His family story is a common one – like Cristina's parents, his grand-parents migrated north in search of work in the 1950s. His father was born in Barcelona but went back to his roots, to Marinaleda, to find work when the struggle for land began, and soon met Ezequiel's mother, from Estepa. 'A lot of people never came back to the south,' Javi explained.

Ezequiel had returned to his parents' house because he had a couple of days off from his job working in a Seville hotel reception, and greeted us warmly – cheeky smiles swim near the surface of the Andalusian gene pool. The house was lovely; modest but big enough, clean but lived-in. Each of the 350 *casitas* built under Sánchez Gordillo's leadership consists of ninety square meters for construction and 100 square meters for a patio or garden, and normally incorporates three bedrooms, a bathroom, living room, kitchen and courtyard. The living room was dominated by a towering bookcase and a large cage of chirruping birds. 'Say "Gordillo"!' Javi instructed a parrot, pointing a finger at it mock sternly. The parrot looked at him impassively and puffed its chest out. 'Say "communism"!' The bird refused.

Ezequiel is one of many young *marinaleños* torn between utopia and the wider world. He wanted to do something more exciting than farming, he explained, whatever the benefits of the co-operative might be. He spent most of the week working in the hotel in Seville, improving his English, renting a small room in a flat there, but even so hadn't quite cut the apron-strings to utopia: he was still coming back to stay at his parents' house most weeks and was on the waiting list to build a *casita* of his own in Marinaleda, in spite of his wanderlust. A fifteen-euro-a-month 'mortgage' for a brand-new house in his *pueblo*, especially in the context of the Spanish housing crisis, would be pretty hard to argue with.

Did you like it, growing up here? I asked him. 'Sure. But if you don't want to work in the fields, what do you do?' What indeed. You probably have to leave for the big city or the coast. Do people here grow up as communists? I wondered. He seemed unsure of what to say. 'Many people become communists, because they want to work, or they want to have a house, but not because they *are* communist. They don't sit at home reading Karl Marx.'

In a way, Ezequiel was no different than any Spaniard of his age – more enticed by the possibilities of gallivanting and adventure than by Sánchez Gordillo's earnest poems about struggle. His parents came back from Catalunya to join the revolution, he acknowledged. 'Ah, but this generation, they don't care about communism,' interrupted Javi, mocking Ezequiel for his ideological heresy. There was some truth to Javi's jibe, and I heard it said more than once in the village, and in the surrounding *pueblos*, that those who inherited utopia may not treat it with the same reverence as those who struggled to create it.

And yet, even with Ezequiel, it felt like a certain level of solidarity had been unconsciously embedded: despite his middling English, he wanted to practice, and told a lucid English-language version of the history of the land seizures that had happened before he was born. The Duke of Infantado, he said, was 'just walking around with a horse, while people starved in Marinaleda'. And then he reeled off the word 'expropriated' without a second thought.

Most English people don't know the word 'expropriated', I told him.

5

Bread and Roses

With the exception of the ferocious heat of high summer, Marinaleda feels at its most utopian in the afternoon. *La tarde* starts not at noon, but when work starts winding down and lunch and siesta time commence, between 2 and 4 pm. The village's few shops and workshops close, workers drift back from the fields and the factory, the pensioners finish their games of cards, and parents stand outside the primary school gates, chatting idly as the kids run in circles around their legs.

Some stop off for a drink on their way home and sip small glasses of beer called *cañitas* (normally about a third of a pint) under the sun-gazebo in front of Bar Gervasio and at the tables outside Bar Sur. Lunch, which never starts before 3 pm, is normally a long-drawn-out affair involving several courses, with loaves of bread broken up into big hunks sitting on the table next to platters of grilled chicken or pork, rich stews of lentils and beans, fanned triangles of manchego and bowls of pale, watery lettuce, tossed with tuna and sweetcorn.

Home is where the stomach is, but the social centre of the Spanish *pueblo*, as Julian Pitt-Rivers observed in his book *The People of the Sierra*, is outdoors, in the streets themselves. During *la tarde*, the broad, tree-lined promenade that runs next to the Avenida de la Libertad, connecting Marinaleda to nearby Matarredonda, is teeming with activity. Gaggles of middle-aged women walk four abreast, men just turning grey jog in pairs, and teenage boys on bikes do that half-standing, half-cycling soft-pedal thing that only teenage boys can pull off, while the girls walk behind them, laughing. The older youths are kitted out as cool young sportsmen, and pose with their lightweight motorbikes, or lean on car doors showing off their tracksuits, like aspiring alpha males everywhere.

After lunch and a short siesta, the heat of the day cools, and the performance is repeated. The pensioners rest their walking sticks against the metal green benches, stocky men stroll two by two in their berets, serious trousers and olive-coloured cardigans, always nattering away, the birds in the surrounding orange trees by now engaged in deep debate too. Outside the *casitas* kids walk their dogs and chase their footballs, and a group of roller-skating tweens flies down the Avenida and into the village park, past the outdoor gym, which is populated by grown-ups doing their work-outs and children using it as a climbing frame. The younger children sit on their mothers' laps on the benches, eating crisps. If you do a circuit of the village, by the time you return half an hour

later the congregations around each bench have rear-
ranged slightly, but the principle remains.

Between the Ayuntamiento and Matarredonda a lush
green field spreads motionless in the afternoon sunshine,
only occasionally disturbed by the two white horses graz-
ing in it. When the sun finally sets, it does so in a blaze of
pink over El Rubio to the west, casting an irresistible peach
glow over the whitewashed walls of the town, with Estepa
sitting prettily on the balcony of the mountains to the
south. When there is more than, say, 50 per cent cloud
coverage, which there very rarely is, dusk is a moodier
affair of purplish, deep-sea blues, but no less picturesque.

'We have every reason to keep fighting', proclaims a
slightly torn Sánchez Gordillo election poster still clinging
to the wall of the *parque natural*. It's not just their work, but
their lifestyle that they're fighting to keep – and in almost
every instance, it's one that they created from the space
they won for themselves: not just via the economically
empowering struggle for land, but by deliberately building
the infrastructure for a cultural and social life far out of
proportion with their size.

The Gordillistas never miss an opportunity to remind
people of the connection between the *marinaleño* quality of
life and *la lucha*. 'You truly believe that without struggle
we could achieve all this?' demanded the central spread of
the 2011 election manifesto brochure, illustrating such
achievements with countless pictures of high days and
holidays, community activities, sports teams and facilities,

and organised fun for children, pensioners and everyone in between.

When the streets are your social centre, it's important to keep them clean. All the house facades are immaculate, the majority of them gleaming white, with only a few rogues in yellow or orange, or covered in beautiful Moorish mosaic tiles. On a morning stroll around the village you'll most likely encounter a few women outside their front doors, sweeping dust and twigs from the pavements. One matriarch beats the front of El Sur with a kind of cat-o'-nine-tails to get the dust out. It still hangs in the air a little, augmenting the hazy sunshine with an extra layer of fuzz. It's a constant struggle, when the motorbikes haring down Avenida de la Libertad are kicking up their own oily smoke too, and the lorries are churning up the dust.

On Sundays, on Calle de Federico García Lorca, one household literally airs its laundry in public, hanging wet linen on a line between the orange trees on the pavement. Nobody minds. Public space is negotiated space, and if someone has a problem with a fellow neighbour's use of it, they will mention it directly. It's too hot in this part of the world to waste time on working yourself up with passive-aggressive grumbling.

If you're not taking the most important meal of the day at home, there's a small range of modest but tremendously cheap tapas dishes in the bars of the village, usually costing one euro each, same as the beers, the glasses of wine and the coffees. And just on the very edge of the village, near the road sign which indicates you are entering Marinaleda, is La Bodega – a proper, spacious family restaurant for passing traffic and locals alike. By 3.30 on weekday lunchtimes it's pretty much full, with fifteen or so cars, lorries and tractors parked outside.

Extended families, work associates and groups of retirees eat there often in large groups of more than ten, drinking decent reds and helping themselves from great communal clay pots of chicken and potatoes. Competing with the flamenco-pop on the stereo is a whirring ceiling fan and *The Simpsons*, dubbed, on a TV in a high corner. There's an open fire, an old-fashioned wood-burning heater, a giant, human-being-sized amphora turned into a plant pot, open shelves messily stacked with wine bottles, and hams hanging behind the bar. The atmosphere reflects the gloriously unhurried Andalusian ethic: *no hay bulla*, there's no fuss. Even the *sopa de mariscos*, seafood broth, off the daily *menú del día* takes over thirty minutes to arrive; but if you've got half-broken, briny olives from the local fields, a good book and a sparkling *cañita*, there really is no fuss.

You can eat a long, langorous lunch, but people also head there in the evenings for less formal tapas plates of rich *rabo de toro*, ox tail, *secreto*, a gloriously moist, fat-marbled cut of pork, and *flamenquín*, the peculiar Andalusian hybrid of a scotch egg and a sausage roll. Eating there with Javi and his mates on a Friday night, they taught me the kind of key contemporary Spanish phrases you don't learn in a language

class. Phrases such as *dinero negro*, black money, and that
Rajoy's government had recently offered the nation's
corrupt businesspeople an *amnistía fiscal*. This meant that
they would clean their dirty money, no questions asked, no
charges pressed, only provided they brought it back to Spain
and paid 10 per cent tax on it. And then there was gossip
about the various senior politicians embroiled in various
corruption scandals. I struggled to keep up with which one
was which: there were simply that many cases in the news at
any one time.

After some light dinner like this, at around 9 or 10 pm,
for the younger adults (and many of the older ones) weekend nights mean more drinks, gently sliding along from
bar to bar, either in the village or a neighbouring *pueblo*,
and eventually some dancing.

In terms of decibel levels Marinaleda is generally a quiet
village, but when they celebrate, they do so in a manner
which is once again far out of proportion to their size. The
major annual festivals – most of them Catholic in origin,
now stripped of all religious rituals and icons – draw in
thousands of outside visitors, from neighbouring villages
and beyond: chiefly the pre-Lenten *carnaval* blow-out, the
week-long July *feria*, and Holy Week recast as *semana
cultural*. In addition there are the famous spring and summer
rock concerts, either in Palo Palo or outdoors in the *feria*
grounds, which frequently see the village double in size.

Sport and physical activity are treated with similar
enthusiasm. Marinaleda has a number of football teams for

different ages and levels – including Unión Deportiva Marinaleda, founded in 1986, which until recently punched above its weight, in the Spanish fourth division. There is also a large outdoor swimming pool, four tennis courts, an indoor gym, an outdoor gym, and in the 500-capacity multi-purpose sports pavilion (the huge white building adorned with Che Guevara's face), basketball, volleyball, gymnastics, judo and handball, among other things. On summer evenings, films are screened – for free, of course – at the purpose-built amphitheatre that sits tucked away in the *parque natural*. Several hundred *marinaleños* bring cushions, food and drink from home, and settle in for the night, while the kids scamper around in the vicinity. All of these, it must be said, are achievements of the Sánchez Gordillo era.

The citizens of Marinaleda have the leisure opportunities and facilities of a village at least five times its size, and that is no accident; but is their provision a distraction, or a reward?

You'd need an unhealthy level of cynicism to argue for the former. There's an evident and sincere ideological commitment to the socialist maxim 'bread and roses', drawn from the James Oppenheim poem of the same name, and its key line: 'Hearts starve as well as bodies; give us bread, but give us roses!' The struggle of the 1980s was for cultural and spiritual sustenance, as well as land – full hearts, as well as stomachs. Joy, Sánchez Gordillo has often said, is a people's right.

In 1985, as the land occupation campaign intensified, he counter-intuitively tested his philosophy by cancelling the *feria* – the major annual community street festival in all Spanish *pueblos*, often lasting up to a week. The economic situation in the village was so dire, Sánchez Gordillo reasoned, that they could not pretend to celebrate. It sounds like a slightly demagogic and eccentric move, but as ever it was ratified by a general assembly, and the villagers understood its propaganda power. Cancelling the *feria* was deemed a newsworthy event, not just by Sánchez Gordillo, but by the national media.

'Without joy, *la fiesta* is impossible,' Sánchez Gordillo said in a solemn declaration to the press. 'Without work, all we know is hopelessness and despair.'

Of course, not just Marinaleda, but the majority of Spanish society had been denied their fundamental right to joy for decades, throughout the Franco years. One of the first principles of organisation in Marinaleda in the 1970s was to rediscover liberty and autonomy in their cultural and social lives – the same spontaneous cultural catharsis that created the hedonistic creative boom known as *la movida madrileña*. *La movida* saw Madrid make partying and transgression into a political statement. The spirit of liberalisation carried across the arts, but also in the Dionysian spirit of drug decriminalisation and the flourishing of previously repressed subcultures of all types.

There was a grassroots cultural and social rebellion across the country, in reaction to an autocratic regime which had brutalised not just bodies, but souls. In the *Marinaleda: Huelga de Hambre* pamphlet, written in 1980, the authors lament that the Francoists 'wanted to impose on the rest of the Spanish state a distorted Andalusian folklore, in an attempt to build a "Spanish culture", uniform and equal for all. In that way, making a caricature of the Andalusians, it tried to use folkloric elements to crush the different cultural manifestations of the *pueblos*.'

This desperate desire to recover local and personal cultural autonomy from repressive central control – control from outside the *pueblo* – was integral to the revolutionary mindset of the late 1970s. As the green-and-white-flag-waving Andalusian nationalists are the first to admit, there is no uniform Andalusian culture, any more than there is a singular Spanish culture. Every *pueblo* has its own unique character, rituals and festivities – and with Franco dead and his architecture of centralised repression crumbling, these began to thrive anew.

For Sánchez Gordillo it was necessary in the late 1970s to pro-actively '*recuperar fiestas*', to reclaim their festivities from the hands of their traditional enemies; Franco, the state, the pro-regime bourgeoisie, and perhaps more controversially, the Catholic Church. In Andalusia, Easter week, or *semana santa*, generally involves an almost total shut-down of normal life for the sake of prayers, processions and other rituals. So while in Seville, dramatically hooded penitents dubbed *naẓarenos* honour the story of Christ's Passion by following their ornate religious icons on ten-hour-long processions, often barefoot, through the medieval city streets, things in Marinaleda are determinedly secular. Sánchez Gordillo's *semana cultural* is an alternative, non-religious celebration, consisting of concerts and theatrical performances.

The current design of Marinaleda's July *feria* is at once an ancient form of community revelry and a conscious subversion of the typical *feria* under Franco: demure fairs in fenced-off grounds, with entry fees which were prohibitive for all but the petty bourgeoisie (small landowners, doctors, priests) and members of the Guardia Civil. These days, of course, the fences have come down, in every sense. Each *feria* is given a new political theme to tie the aesthetics together, which is decided at a general assembly: previous themes have included agrarian reform, the current housing crisis, and Che Guevara.

The *feria* is a political festival in these relatively superficial leftist flourishes, but its politics run deeper: it couldn't happen without the largely voluntary work and enthusiasm of the collective. Several hundred volunteers serve food and drink, construct the stages, and prepare villagers of all ages – and incomes – for a boozy week of free entertainment and dancing until way beyond dawn.

Marinaleda's notoriety as a cultural jewel of the Sierra Sur is also a good source of income for the village, or the SAT union, depending on who is officially behind each event. One high-profile fundraising concert on the outdoor *feria* grounds in February 2013 sold 5,000 tickets at fifteen euros each (the population is 2,700, remember). Billed as a 'Concert Against Repression', its posters were plastered across the entire region. All the proceeds went to the SAT legal fighting fund, following numerous arrests during the previous year's many strikes and pieces of direct action.

As well as bringing money into the village, these kinds of festivities make pretty good publicity for the project. Elsewhere in Andalusia I have met people who've come to Marinaleda just for the gigs or the *feria* – even one or two who know the town primarily for its parties, rather than its politics. The emphasis on bread and roses is both a useful supplement to propaganda and something grounded in Sánchez Gordillo's sincere belief in the betterment of the collective:

'We believe that public well-being should never have a limit,' he told me in 2012. 'Private well-being should. But public well-being, the good of everyone – not some more than others – the well-being of a collectivity; that should be limitless.' He then reeled off a list of facilities, indexed by price: 'Wireless internet is free. Swimming in the public pool costs three euros for the entire year. The child daycare centre costs twelve euros a month – and the children also eat there.' Many of these amenities have come directly through protest. When I met Sánchez Gordillo the first time, he was talking about the next addition to the leisure life of Marinaleda, an indoor swimming pool complex for which artists' designs had already been agreed. If the Junta was unwilling to foot the bill, they would just have to protest until it gave way, he said.

Marinaleda's relationship with the state is a curious web of paradoxes. They despise its intrusions, its determination to throttle their liberty, rights and local culture, and its historic enmity to the autonomous spirit of the *pueblo*; but they still make appeals to the central state, as well as to the regional government – more than that, they make strident, substantial financial demands of it – and simultaneously call it names, disrupt its functions and repeatedly, determinedly, break its laws. All of which makes it the more astonishing that neither the Andalusian nor the Spanish government objected to Sánchez Gordillo's dramatic-sounding decision to abolish the police force.

'They didn't say anything!' he insisted. 'By law, due to the number of inhabitants we have here, we should have around four to seven cops. But we don't want police here. The one policeman we had wasn't allowed to have a gun. Then when he retired, he wasn't thrown out of the village or anything – but we didn't hire a new policeman, because we don't need one. Because we have our voluntary work, because we throw a lot of parties and party collectively, because we fight together, because we make our lives together, there is a high degree of good neighbourliness. When we plant trees, we do that together, too.'

Sánchez Gordillo's articulation of what the word 'community' means is especially striking when you consider how blithely and emptily the word is used by mainstream politicians across the West.

Suspicion of the state, of any extension of centralised power, is something that flourishes in the Andalusian soil – and has been especially intensified in Marinaleda, thanks to its unique three decades of struggle. Of course, there is always the Guardia Civil. You see them slowly driving down Avenida de la Libertad sometimes, suspicious sentinels of a remote but destructive power, patrolling in their green and white cars, still adorned with the emblem of the royal crown over a sword crossed with a *fasces*.

The young lads standing outside the bars purse their lips or mutter obscenities, careful not to do so too loudly. The Guardia still have jurisdiction, as Spain's national gendarmerie; the local station is in Herrera, six miles away. Hypothetically, if there was a sudden and vicious murder, it would be members of this Guardia who would be summoned to deal with it.

In 2007, the Herrera force was called in after repeated robberies and vandalism at the two schools in Marinaleda. A small group, largely suspected to be a few students with discipline problems who rarely attended class, had stolen pieces of sports equipment from the school and left a trail of broken glass, forced doors and windows, and walls daubed with insults aimed at their teachers.

Normally, if there's this kind of trouble, they don't let it get as far as the Guardia. I heard one story of a group of local youngsters committing acts of boredom-inspired petty vandalism, throwing stones and blowing up letter-boxes with fireworks, so the residents on the street affected spoke to Sánchez Gordillo, who gave them his mobile number and told them to call if it happened again. It did, and they called him at 11 pm one night. He turned up five minutes later in a car, and the kids scarpered; but he worked out who they were, went and talked to their parents, and it never happened again.

The young people do get bored sometimes, as they do in small villages everywhere. Weed is smoked slyly, and not so slyly, in the fields away from the grown-ups, or in a huddle on the Casa de Cultura staircase. Other recrea-tional activities not permitted in parents' homes have caused problems. On one recent visit, while taking a stroll, I noticed a sign affixed to the allotment and garden situated next to the school. 'This park is for enjoying, not fucking', it said, dispensing with any attempt at euphemism. The young people can get bored, but – and it's a 'but' acknowl-edged by them and their parents alike – it could be so much worse. They have innumerable sporting options, free Wi-Fi at home, a park and swimming pool to hang out in, free computers in the Casa de Cultura internet café, and in general, a hell of a lot more going on than in most villages of fewer than 3,000 people. And when they grow up they have the possibility of work and home ownership denied to the majority of their peers elsewhere in Spain.

Their grandparents are certainly well occupied, not least in the Centro de Adultos, where, among other things,

literacy classes provide education for an older generation that never had the chance to complete formal schooling. It's also a social hub, especially popular with the village's older women. There's even a thrice-weekly evening class in Spanish for the village's émigrés, mostly Brits plus the odd Frenchman, Romanian and Senegalese. The evening classes are all brought together for termly day-trips to regional sites of interest, like the Alhambra in Granada. During one of my visits, I was invited to a pre-Christmas meal where the women made us *migas*, a popular peasant dish consisting entirely of mounds and mounds of fried breadcrumbs – served with wedges of fresh orange to cut through all the oil. It felt as heavy and dense as the dirt in the fields; but again, I hadn't spent all day working in them, so probably hadn't built up the right kind, or volume, of appetite. For dessert we were served another delicacy, *gachas dulces* – which again looked rather like gloop, tasted rather like gloop, weighed a tonne and, all told, was quite pleasant.

After we'd finished eating, the old ladies tried to get the last few breadcrumbs off the plates by smacking the back of them with plastic spoons – a deafening impromptu percussion section, accompanied by plenty of giggling. Following an earlier discussion about *leche frita*, a kind of deep-fried custard, one of the teachers, Rafa, a kindly man in his late thirties with a childlike sensibility, beamed and led the old ladies in a chant of '*¡Queremos leche frita! ¡Queremos leche frita!*' (we want *leche frita*!). They banged their plates in time as the chants grew louder, before finally dissolving into laughter. 'This is what it's like all the time,' said *la inglesa* Ali, fondly, with a smile and an eye-roll. 'If the lunatics ever do take over the asylum, this is what it'll look like.'

After things settled down again, I pulled out my *Huelga de Hambre* book, and they crowded round to look at the pictures. Like the veterans of *la lucha* in the olive oil factory, they'd never seen them before. There was again a great deal of reminiscing about the assemblies, the hunger and the heat, the friends who had since passed on. Hands clapped brows: what a strange, distant place August 1980 was. They have created a remarkable world since then, but they grew up in one, too. One older woman in the class recalled giving birth to her third child, out in the fields; the defining characteristic about this particular birth, the thing that jogged her memory, was not that it happened in the middle of a field – an unsurprising detail – but that it was raining that day. 'Oh yes!' responded her friend, 'it *was* raining that day.'

Afterwards, Rafa took me to see the village library in the building opposite. I asked about village archives, and he said regretfully there wasn't really anything at all. We leafed through the official Ayuntamiento de Andalucía statistics almanacs, the kind of dry tome that every local library has, but there is no proper archive available to the villagers. There weren't many political books at all, in fact, let alone any specific to the Andalusian struggle: only a lonely copy of Lenin's *¿Qué hacer?* (*What Is to Be Done?*).

For a village and a region with such an extraordinary history, it's remarkably under-historicised. In the Ayuntamiento, there are no meaningful archives either. 'It's surprising, I know,' one amiable employee, Manolo, told me, 'not least because local government is so bureaucratic!' Directly downstairs from the library is the pensioners' social club, where the old men drink one-euro coffees and *cañitas*, read the newspapers, and play cards most of the day. The history is with them, passed down the generations through storytelling and the reproduction of the practice of struggle, rather than upstairs in the library.

One local organisation that does keep records of its activities – and publishes them in a magazine-like bulletin – is the institution that has had a guiding hand throughout so much of Spanish history: the Church. You wouldn't think they had much of a history in Marinaleda since 1979, if you read any of the short online pieces about the village. Indeed, when I asked him about Christian festivities and the village's attitude to Catholic tradition and faith, Sánchez Gordillo told me confidently: 'We are not religious.' Even at the time, this seemed a bit of a presumptuous generalisation. Almost every village in Spain, however small, has a church – Marinaleda has two, in fact, one in each barrio. 'Yes, there is a church,' he admitted, in a manner that suggested I had missed the point, 'but there's no priest. Priests are dangerous. We like to say, "Thank God we have no priest."'

In reality, unsurprisingly, erasure of Catholicism from the workers' credo espoused by Sánchez Gordillo since

1979 did not have the effect of erasing all of that faith which existed before. And so, in spite of his statement that 'we' are not religious, and the fact that the *semana cultural* has ostensibly replaced *semana santa*, both worship in general and that vital part of the Spanish Catholic year, Holy Week, continue in Marinaleda.

The Catholic Easter traditions persist in the streets of the *pueblo*, starting with the Palm Sunday procession in which children walk dressed as apostles, accompanied by one *niño* dressed as Jesus Christ on his donkey. It proceeds on Good Friday with the parading of the Christ statue from the seventeenth-century Iglesia Parroquial de Nuestra Señora de la Esperanza, tucked away from the main road in the north-western corner of the village, and then the Virgen de la Esperanza, the Virgin of Hope, the village's patron saint. There is also weekly worship with a non-resident priest, Manuel Martínez Valdivieso, who presides in El Rubio. He and Sánchez Gordillo avoid each other, and Valdivieso has been known to say, bitterly, that he is the priest for all of the village, whereas Sánchez Gordillo is only mayor of the half who elected him.

There are half-truths to Sánchez Gordillo's claim that utopia is secular. Marinaleda is certainly much less observant than many neighbouring *pueblos*, and it is, crucially, situated in a long history of often violent enmity between the Church and the workers. The Church has traditionally been a proxy for the State, both before and, in a sense, even after Franco's dictatorship. Until recently, a portion of all

Spaniards' income tax went towards paying for the upkeep of the Catholic Church and the salaries of the clergy; only in 1988 did the PSOE bring in the possibility to opt out by ticking a box on your income tax form.

But the peripatetic priest, Valdivieso, is right too. The regular churchgoers complain, studiously off the record, that they are marginalised by the village's official culture. No one will despise them for going to Mass, much less prevent them from doing so, but it's telling that the Ayuntamiento and the Marinaleda TV station ignore all religious events in the village.

'Holy Week does exist' in Marinaleda, protests the peculiar, ancient-looking website of the parish church, in a declaration surrounded by kitsch religious clip-art, 'and there is a small Brotherhood whose office-holders are highly revered in the village.' The legacy of a time when reverence was more commonplace – indeed, under Franco, at the very heart of state-sanctioned culture – is still visible behind closed doors. Throughout my host Antonio's house, the walls and shelves are crowded with Catholic icons and trinkets, more on the refined than the kitsch side; paintings, figurines, framed passages from the Bible.

When I first arrived, I assumed – wrongly – that their presence must mean Antonio was an anti-Gordillista, as if you had to make a choice: you were either conventionally religious or a worshipper of the new messiah. Chatting one evening after dinner, I discovered he was neither. 'The heavy metal concerts they have for *semana cultural* are very popular here,' he told me from his rocking chair, before getting up to stoke the coals in the fire. I used the opportunity to ask about the icons on the walls. 'No, no, all of these religious things were my mother's, and I just left them up.' Most *marinaleños* have become communists instead of Catholics, he added – it's a direct replacement, a new faith.

Are you a believer in the new religion then? I asked. 'No!' he said, happily. 'I don't like politics either. I believe in nothing – I'm a nihilist, an existentialist. I just want to live, I don't need a philosophy. I have my friends here, and everywhere I go people say hello to me. There's no crime. The police and the priests are superfluous – and so are the politicians.' In this wonderfully charming, slightly camp septuagenarian, it struck me, was the innate Andalusian anarchism I'd read about. Individual freedom and autonomy above all else – and a pox on authority figures of all kinds.

'*Carnaval* is my favourite holiday of the whole year,' Cristina had told me with genuine excitement a few months beforehand, 'better than Christmas, better than s*emana cultural*, better than the *feria*.' It's the traditional Catholic pre-Lenten festival, a last gasp of indulgence before forty days of self-sacrifice; in Marinaleda, they persist with the festivity, but without the religious penitence that follows. In the run-up to carnival, the only discussion is your *disfraz*, your costume. Like a ludic version of anarchist 'affinity groups' convened for direct action, in groups of up to fifteen close friends, they choose a collective theme and work on their costumes together.

This was carnival season across the *pueblos* of the Sierra Sur, and there was an ineffable excitement in the air. There seemed to be a greater than usual number of boy racers roaring down Avenida de la Libertad, playing reggaeton so loud it shakes my bedroom window. On the Saturday before Lent, Estepa, Rubio, Herrera and all the rest of the surrounding villages celebrate, with two exceptions. In midweek, Pedrera has its unique Ash Wednesday *carnaval*. The following Saturday, after the start of Lent, and thus somewhat missing the point of a pre-Lenten bacchanal, is Marinaleda's turn. The date was chosen for the simple reason that they want everyone in the region to come, rather than competing with all the other festivities.

When I attended in 2013, the revels began with a parade around the village: everyone was told to congregate at 7 pm on Saturday night, in the Ayuntamiento car park. I arrived early – which is to say, on time – but even with only a quarter of the participants there, it was already quite a scene.

The people who dress up are mostly between the ages of five and thirty-five – liable therefore to get excitably drunk on either rum-and-coke or plain coke, depending. Every group wheels around a trolley stocked to the brim with bottles of booze, mixers and plastic cups. There were swarms of bugs, squirrels and harlequins, about twelve aliens in green body paint and purple wigs, a good showing of clowns, doctors and nurses, a few hens, some slightly dubious geishas and Native Americans, straw men from the Wizard of Oz, a bullfighter or two, and a gaggle of hippies. As the crowd swelled with ever more ridiculous-looking incomers, the older people of the village gathered around the edges of the car park, looking on in their serious brown and grey civvies; parents proudly arranged their little ones for photos. Even before we set off on the hour-long, slow-step circuit around almost every street in the village, there was already a high fever of singing, extravagant toasts to each other and to the village, and giddy high jinks. The human right to joy was exercised with righteous determination: it was a tremendous piss-up.

There were prizes for the best group costume, and some displayed their theme with impressive thoroughness. One group had built a large, mobile, mostly cardboard elephant to embellish their big-game hunting theme. Topically, it featured the Spanish king Juan Carlos I in camouflage greens, who gave an interview in character to Marinaleda TV, surrounded by his fellow hunters, and, awkwardly, a couple of 'natives' in grass skirts and blackface. The man dressed as the king looked so uncannily like the real Juan Carlos that I hardly recognised him at first – it was Bigotes from the olive oil factory, but crucially, shockingly, without his talismanic moustache: he had shaved it off for the occasion.

There were also two young men dressed as Mexican bandits, who made up for their slightly hackneyed outfits by riding actual animals, one a white horse, the other a donkey. But best of all, only a week after Benedict XVI announced his resignation, was the papal entourage. The pope himself, smoking cheap cigarettes and drinking vodka and coke from a fake golden goblet, was driven around in an actual functioning Popemobile, converted from a golf cart, piloted by one of his equally lairy cardinals.

The image that will stay in my head longest is that of a little girl dressed all in black, with a *V for Vendetta*–style Guy Fawkes mask, of the kind popularised by Occupy, drinking a carton of orange juice through a straw, her black cape gently floating behind her. She was in an all-female troupe of more than ten Guy Fawkeses of various ages and heights, who'd even dressed their trolley in black. The legacy of old-school anti-establishment militancy, filtered through pop culture, into the ancient rite of costuming.

After the parade, people settled around the nucleus of Palo Palo, Gervasio, the Sindicato bar and Disco Pub Jesa for a long night of eating, drinking and dancing. Temporary stalls and food vans sold band t-shirts, sweets, kebabs and waffles. The under-twenty-ones established their own area around the back of the Sindicato, to drink away from their parents, smoke dope, and mill about like teenagers do to three different car-boot sound-systems, blaring cheesy techno, the inevitable reggaeton, and Gangnam Style, this last seemingly on a loop. Disco Pub Jesa was home to a lot more cheesy global pop music and a lot more dancing – even intergenerational dancing – while directly outside it, tied to a lamppost, stood a donkey. While the parents drank, many of their young children were still up and about, playing football in their costumes into the small hours. Indeed, at 2 am there were still as many actual prams outside the bars as there were drunk men in their late twenties dressed up as babies.

Even at that time, more revellers were turning up from other villages, some of them in costume. The latest point at which I managed to have a serious conversation about the village was around midnight in the Sindicato bar, according to my increasingly illegible notes. Paco, a smart, serious man in early middle age, was even-handed in his appraisal of the village: 'The crisis is not just here, but everywhere . . . this can be a beacon for the world if we remake it and start again. A new utopia, a different one.'

'When I first came back to Marinaleda from Barcelona [in the 1980s], I came to an assembly and his words got me, here,' Paco said, patting his chest.

Organised fun is integral to the spirit of the *pueblo*, but so is the less organised kind. On a Thursday night in December, the night before Constitution Day, a national holiday, I went out for a quiet drink with a friend at 10 pm. There were only about seven people in Bar Gervasio: two young women, and a separate group of five men in their early twenties. The football was on, the fire was substantial and warm, and not much was happening. As the hours passed, the lads were knocking back not light, sensible *cañas* but *copas*, large glasses containing something like three, four or five shots of hard spirits (who knows, since they never, ever, measure in this part of the world), topped up with coke or lemonade.

By midnight they had persuaded Gervasio, the owner, to switch the cables so as to broadcast music videos from his laptop behind the bar onto the big TV. By 2 am the drink and carefree, what-the-hell atmosphere of the village at large had persuaded not just the five lads, but the rest of us too, to get up and dance 'La Macarena', complete with every one of the silly choreographed moves, hip thrusts and twists. *La lucha*, the way Sánchez Gordillo tells it, is a solemn fight to achieve those moments where the inherent, irrepressible dignity of the people finally triumphs. This was not, perhaps, one of those moments.

Cheesy pop music is enduringly popular in this part of the world, and after an equally rumbunctious sing-along and dance-along to Whigfield's 'Saturday Night', we were treated to La Macarena's less local contemporary equivalent, 'Gangnam Style' by Psy. I shouldn't have been surprised, but it did feel striking that a pop phenomenon from South Korea was that familiar to the denizens of a village so isolated thirty years ago that its mayor compared it to a Native American reservation, an island in a sea of *latifundios*. Most of these young men's grandparents had never seen the sea, one hour's drive to the south, much less rejoiced – dance moves and all – in the music of a country 10,000 km away.

It was followed by a popular Spanish Gangnam parody about the cuts, entitled *En el paro estoy*, I'm on the dole. Mouthing the kind of lyrics common to everyday conversation – 'I don't know what to do anymore', 'I moved back in with my parents', 'my grandmother can't go to bingo', 'my girlfriend left me', a sarcastically grinning young man in a yellow reflective jacket and protective helmet goes around doing Psy's cowboy dance and picking up euros off the floor in desperation. 'Rajooooy, give me work!' runs the chorus. Parodying something which is already a parody is fairly low-level art, and it hasn't got the deep-set pain of blues or indeed, more relevantly, flamenco, but it obviously touched a nerve with the 9 million people who viewed it on YouTube.

Later, slightly tired from all the excitement, the young men in the bar switched away from music, re-stocked their rum and cokes, and cued up YouTube clips from a Catalan sketch show called *Polònia*, the one about *el Régimen de Franco*, or the Franco Regime. Since *régimen* means both regime and slimming diet, the conceit is a spoof advert from the old days, in flickering black-and-white, in which an effete, over-eager General Franco advertises his regime like a diet. With the Franco regime, you can't eat meat in Easter week, you can't have sex, you can't smoke pot, you can't speak Catalan; and all of this will bring you guaranteed weight loss. Follow this diet, it concludes, '*para tener mejor facha*', for a better look – a pun on the other sense of *facha*, short for fascist.

At some point closer to 4 am than midnight, Gervasio disappeared into a back room and re-emerged a little later dressed in the unmistakable outfit of the Guardia Civil, complete with bizarre green tricorne hat. The young men fell about laughing, and when they'd picked themselves up off the floor, jostled to have their photos taken with him.

The costume was a caricature, Cristina explained the following night, laughing at my photo of her wasted young peers, thumbs up, posing with the pretend Guardia. It was mockery, not an affectionate tribute to the enemies of the people. It was also related to it being the eve of Constitution Day: a day that celebrates Madrid, and the central state, epitomised by the Guardia. Caricature is a popular form, as the Cadiz *carnaval* testifies.

There was another custom Gervasio practised that I was fond of. Cristina and I had just paid our tab after a slightly quieter evening in his bar – you always pay at the end of the night – when a fresh round of drinks arrived at the table. I was confused: I had thought we were leaving. It turned out that Gervasio had 'invited' us. Crisis or no crisis, the bar owners often do this in Marinaleda: you pay, and one more round arrives, on the house.

The landlord at Palo Palo, León, was king of these extravagantly generous invitations; I lost count of the number of drinks I had on the house with him. His bar is one of the key landmarks in the town, open for over a decade now, and famous far beyond the village, thanks to its mix of high-profile gigs and eccentric Wild West theme, complete with fake logs around the walls and saloon doors. Its exterior is if anything even more striking: above the broad entrance is a fifty-foot-long guitar, whose base is shaped exactly like the map of Andalusia.

Palo Palo specializes in rock music, booking bands with such illustrious names as DP Ebola and Anvil of Doom. As one critic sarcastically complained, 'They have broad taste at Palo: punk, hard metal, dark metal, Satanic metal.' It's not entirely fair.

León took a liking to me the first time he met me, when an English filmmaker, Uzma, was visiting too. He came around the bar to join us for shot after shot of sweet rum liquor (on the house, at his insistence). As the clock ticked gently past 3 am, he swayed to the live blues guitarist's mixture of French, Spanish and English rock and pop – playing to a crowd of less than ten.

León dragged the ashtray over and leaned in closer, drunker, to tell us that Andalusia is a nation without borders, with many different people and cultures – it's the place of the Moors, too. He said it proudly, and it wasn't the first time I had heard *marinaleños* speak that way of their ancestry as Al-Andalus, as well as Andalusia. He was probably showing off to Uzma a bit, since she had ancestors from the Indian subcontinent and was a relatively rare non-white face in the village, but he meant it, too. 'No borders!' he exclaimed. 'For me, it's just people.' He brought up Israel and Palestine, India and Pakistan, Spain and Morocco. They're all brothers and sisters, he said.

As talk turned to politics, he oscillated between finger-jabbing seriousness and rocking back on his bar stool, laughing a big toothy grin. 'I'm not a socialist, or a communist,' he announced eventually, wagging his index finger. 'Then what is your philosophy – what are we drinking to?' I asked.

He reeled back, swung around to grab the next round of sweet caramel rum and raised it with outstretched arm, as if to make a big announcement to the room, to the world at large.

'*La libertad.*'

6

Opposition in Utopia

Mariano Pradas asked to meet us on the very edge of Matarredonda, where the smaller end of the village drops suddenly away into open fields, and Avenida de la Libertad splits into two, south towards Estepa, or east towards Herrera. We parked on a dirt layby next to the junction, and since it was a gloriously sunny day, we got out and stood by the car until he turned up. It felt like waiting to do a drug deal, or a hostage exchange. Passengers in passing cars turned their heads to glance curiously at the four young men idling on the edge of the village in the middle of the afternoon – I had brought along Javi, from Estepa, Ezequiel, from Marinaleda, and Dave, my photographer friend from London.

Eventually Mariano pulled up, parked alongside us and got out, shaking hands with everyone, cautiously friendly, but formal. Then we got back in our cars, and followed him through the winding olive groves out of town. After fifteen minutes or so he indicated a turning, a rocky dirt track cut right into the middle of the groves – so narrow that I could have reached out the window and picked the olives off the trees. The path wound slowly and bumpily up a gentle incline, to a cottage located behind high wire mesh fences topped with barbed wire. 'Wow. I guess this is the opposition compound?' muttered Dave, only partially in jest, as three dogs jumped up to the gate. One was massive, two were almost comically tiny, which took the edge off the slight atmosphere of unease.

In the cottage, we sat down at the kitchen table, and Mariano rolled up one blind above the sink. We remained in this dim half-light for the couple of hours we sat there and talked. It was only a simulacrum, but we really felt like we were in hiding.

I had got the sense that Mariano Pradas is rather unfairly maligned in Marinaleda, where he is one of two elected Socialist Party (PSOE) councillors, alongside the nine of Sánchez Gordillo's Izquierda Unida (IU). He tends to slink around town. On the night of Marinaleda's February carnival, while I was having dinner with friends in one of the less popular (and thus conveniently emptier) village cafés, Mariano came in on his own, looked around slightly shiftily, had a quick, quiet conversation with the grumpy, boss-eyed owner, and crept off again. He and the other PSOE councillor, José Rodríguez Cobacho, rarely join in with any of the community's cultural events: they say they don't feel welcome. Crucially, neither of them actually live in Marinaleda itself; they're both up the hill in Estepa.

To commence his victory speech after the local elections in 2012, Sánchez Gordillo announced to the waiting crowd, as if delivering the football scores, 'Marinaleda 9, Estepa 2' – and was met with enormous cheers. Little could better elucidate the incredible persistence of that key facet of Andalusian life: you are your *pueblo*, and as long as the PSOE representatives live in Estepa, their dedication to and understanding of the life of Marinaleda will be called into question.

Pradas would counter, fairly, that he was born in Marinaleda, he grew up there, and his family are from there. He remembers the bad old days, the daily struggle of life under the dictatorship, and his analysis of the dire state the village was in before the 1980s isn't that different from Sánchez Gordillo's – a desperately poor *pueblo* surrounded by *latifundios*, and a people heedlessly left to starve by a political elite with no interest in them.

I was curious to know how anyone from the PSOE, a nominally socialist party, would even begin to make a case against the *jornaleros*' long, successful fight for the land. Sure enough, Pradas was careful not to dismiss the struggle, or the land occupations. 'In part, it was a good thing,' he said, in an I-hold-my-hands-up sort of way. 'The *jornaleros* have some land now, and that's a good thing. But it doesn't provide everyone with as much work as they claim. There is not full employment here, not even close – the real problem is the lack of industry in Andalusia.' The CUT/SAT fixation on winning the land was a myopic obsession, the way he told the story of the 1980s: 'A lot of different things are necessary to make progress,' he explained, 'not just fields.'

What about the hunger strike, I asked. 'The truth?' He laughed a little, involuntarily: not derisive, or disrespectful, but an irreverent laugh, directed at the legend built up around it. 'The truth is, it has been massively sentimentalised. The majority of people had nothing to do with it.' He repeated Félix Talego's analysis, that it was first and foremost a well-orchestrated media event, coordinated from the top by Sánchez Gordillo with the help of the union and the party.

'Marinaleda is a divided *pueblo*. Sánchez Gordillo has worked hard to make sure it is divided, using the assemblies, the TV station, and so on. If you are not on his side, that puts you on the right, that makes you a fascist – and you are attacked, you are insulted, you are intimidated.' Their first task, he said, if the PSOE won control of the village council, would be to restore freedom of thought, and let people make their own decisions, without the polarity of being either 'pro' or 'anti' the mayor. They would consider questions of how to run El Humoso, and all the other aspects of Sánchez Gordillo's Marinaleda, after that.

Sure, Pradas said, you have a secret ballot, and a free vote – but it's the other aspects of life in the village which are undemocratic: people know if you are with Sánchez Gordillo or not. 'If you're not clearly a fanatic, people assume you are the other way.' And the assemblies? 'They are only a superficial expression of democracy. Those who are not Gordillistas would never bother going in the first place, and those who are, are mostly attending because they know it will help them get work in El Humoso.' It is, he said, no different from the era of the *caciques* – the informal biases, the distribution of work and favours to people on 'the right side'.

It is both known and noted whether you are participating in demonstrations and strikes. If you do, you're in line for favours, and if you don't, you're a fascist.

'Intimidation doesn't have to be physical,' he said, solemnly. 'Many people have felt uncomfortable, and had to leave the village for Estepa or elsewhere.'

In the past, he said, his sister's house in the village had had 'fascist' and 'criminal' daubed on the door. Pradas himself had been called a fascist by Sánchez Gordillo in council meetings; he'd had his car vandalised 'for political reasons'. The accusations kept coming. During one episode of *Línea Directa*, his Saturday TV programme, the mayor said that anyone who wanted to celebrate *semana santa* with a procession was a fascist. 'He thinks religious people must be fascists – you can't be on the left and religious, apparently. He talks about freedom a lot, but where is the religious freedom? Personally, I don't believe in much either, but I respect the tradition of *semana santa*.'

As with so many of the allegations and counter-allegations, unpicking the gossip from the facts is almost impossible. There are a few verified incidents: in

November 1986, a group of fifty *marinaleños* broke the windows and scratched the bodywork of the regional PSOE leadership's cars when they came to open a party headquarters in the village.

After the interview we climbed up on a rickety ladder to stand on Pradas's roof and look out to the horizons. As we chatted and looked in vain for discernible landmarks amid the rolling hills, I noticed his consonants were being swallowed up in his round, slightly forlorn face: a word like *después* sinking into his cheeks and becoming '*depweh*'. He was a funny character, near but not quite at the end of his tether as the figurehead of '*la oposición*'. He alternated between slight exhaustion and faint amusement when recounting his arguments with the Gordillistas – essentially the same arguments they'd been having for decades. As was true in the time of the *caciques*, much of it came down to personal tensions between him and his opponent. I asked what he thought would have happened if Sánchez Gordillo had never got involved in politics: would someone else have picked up the same mantle? Will this project continue when he is no longer mayor?

'Definitely not. Gordillismo without Gordillo is impossible,' he said, without a moment's reflection. 'For me his politics aren't even communism, it's a politics very personal to him. After Sánchez Gordillo, business will flourish again. We can all move on.'

*   *   *

Over several decades of struggle, Sánchez Gordillo has established a firm narrative for the Marinaleda story, and you can read this narrative repeated online in countless articles, in many different languages, in near-identical form. They've been engaged in struggle long enough to attract journalists, activists, filmmakers and photographers from almost every country in Europe, and numerous places beyond. It's only after staying for more than a short while, and probing around the edges of the locals' superficial memories, that you start to realise how tightly bound and narrowly focused Sánchez Gordillo's narrative is.

It's not even that there's any malevolent intent to this. Sánchez Gordillo is comparable to a veteran rock star, at the top of his field for decades, who has been compelled to do the same interview over and over again. It's become a bit of a chore, but he can't skip it, because that would be self-defeating, so he reels off the same lines again by rote, the same key points in the narrative: they formed a party and a trade union, went on hunger strike, occupied the fields, won the fields, and built a communist utopia free of crime, police or religion, that provides work, housing and leisure for all. With the best will in the world, it is inevitable that this simple, official narrative is economical with the truth. It's also inevitable that Sánchez Gordillo's critics have been quick to find the holes in it and shout about them.

The Spanish right are fond of describing Marinaleda as a 'communist theme park', a miniature Cuba or North

Korea; a failed micro-state, with Che's face painted over the cracks in its democracy. The land occupations have been described as 'Mugabe-esque', and the leader as an absolutist who does what all communists do: erase individual potential and talent, mowing down the tall poppies with the sickle and bashing the rest of them with the hammer. Apart from anything else, to attack Marinaleda for being a miniature Soviet satellite is to completely ignore the history of the region, and the kind of politics its people have been drawn towards: individual freedom has always been paramount, and so it remains today in the village. It's worth reiterating that Marinaleda follows Spanish electoral law to the letter, yet breaks national laws by having no police force. In a number of the village bars, Spain's smoking ban is simply ignored, and ashtrays sit on the tables. For better or worse, this is anything but a controlling or authoritarian state.

The murals, in their varied litany of global causes, certainly have a Cuban feel to them. They are an expression of a political identity, or range of identities, to locals and visitors alike. They are also, as one critic argued, a secular catechism – a litany of faith to the believers, and a consciously provocative statement to outsiders and infidels. In that five-minute walk down Avenida de la Libertad, you are given a visual summary of the Sánchez Gordillo doctrine: only agrarian reform will end rural poverty; capitalist TV is propaganda; peace cannot come from militarism; Marinaleda remains true to the Spanish Second

Republic, opposes fascism everywhere, and struggles in solidarity with the people of the Basque Country, Catalunya, various parts of South and Central America, Western Sahara, and Palestine.

Some critics of nineteenth-century Andalusian anarchism identified in it a millenarian streak, a replacement of their historical Christian faith with an all-consuming belief that only an inevitable workers' revolution would bring about the new world previously promised to them by the Catholic Church. Arguably a part of that tendency still lingers. You can choose to see this symbolism in the imagery on the village crest and in some of the murals, which depict Marinaleda as a utopian idyll of green fields and clean white houses under a golden sun, a world born anew from the revivifying acts of workers' struggle. But is this imagery really evidence of a messianic, millenarian communism? The fields *are* mostly green, the houses *are* mostly white and the sun *is* relentless, and undeniably yellow.

In an interview with the *Diario de Sevilla* newspaper in November 2011, Sánchez Gordillo said: 'I am a spiritual leader, if you want to call it that.' Certainly, as he said on that occasion, his 'flock' trusts him. The flock has a powerful devotion to the leader, and, when the situation calls for it, a willingness to take physical risks (fighting the Spanish police, for example) to defend the creed he espouses. But this is to stretch a point: Gordillismo is not a cult, much less a millenarian one. Even the criticism of the wall of murals as sinisterly 'Cuban' needs unpacking: they are contributions from all over the world, and not commissioned by the town hall. If this is a catechism, it is an open-source catechism, rather than one dictated from the top.

The Cuban-ness of the mayor's office is perhaps more robustly expressed in that facility that surely every small village needs: its own radio and TV station. They were established in the 1980s and 1990s respectively to provide an alternative to what Sánchez Gordillo calls 'the voice of the master', filtering in from the capitalist media outside.

The Marinaleda media hub is housed between the wall of murals and the Ayuntamiento in the impressive Casa de Cultura, and consists of a few rooms of production desks and edit suites, as well as two dedicated studios. Enlivened with footage of local activities and festivities, demonstrations and rallies, Sánchez Gordillo's topical phone-in show airs every week for an hour and a half. Looming above the banks of dials in the edit suite on my first visit there, the TV screens were all displaying freeze-frame close-ups of the mayor, disrupted in full flow. It was a slightly eye-watering image, the lurid reds and greens in the studio backdrop clashing noisily with Gordillo's bold orange jacket.

Part of this centrepiece phone-in show, *Línea Directa*, is dedicated to local issues, and the rest to the bigger picture: it might be events in Andalusia, or a discussion of Palestine. The inspiration sometimes cited is *Aló Presidente*, the late Hugo Chávez's unscripted talk show, in which he addressed the Venezuelan people at length. In the studio itself, there were chairs set out for the studio audience – although the programme is not the most visual of feasts, usually confined to a static camera on Sánchez Gordillo. Initially the programme lasted three hours, and the production team had to carefully explain to him that this might need cutting down a bit. Sometimes Sánchez Gordillo reads his poetry directly to the camera, intercut with footage of El Humoso's pastoral idyll. The poetry embroiders familiar themes; indeed, he has got into trouble with his critics for lines like 'the right is verily Satan in flesh and blood'.

In my residence the TV was almost always on in the living room, and my host Antonio would occasionally let me flick over from his heavy diet of comically overblown Latin American *telenovelas* to watch a bit of Marinaleda TV. It was usually a series of short clips of recent activities, protests, or information about upcoming sporting activities – register for next month's youth table tennis tournament! That kind of thing. If you live in Marinaleda, you can't really avoid being on TV – if you go on demos, or out during festivals, you'll be filmed.

One fifteen-minute segment recorded the visit of a blue-haired Argentinian hippy, who had come to give the village pensioners a session of New Age dance and physical interaction in the pavilion. Soft music played as she encouraged them to awkwardly stroke each other's faces. This programme sticks in my memory because of Antonio's helpless laughter at the evident discomfort of the participants, his friends and neighbours. Next was a short segment about the recent occupation of empty government farms in Somonte – a big story for SAT, and hence for Marinaleda, accompanied by a medley of Spanish punk and funk. Finally, they filled time with a montage of some women in the vegetable processing factory impassively piling up roasted peppers, de-seeding them, and generally working the production line, accompanied by the blissed-out reggae of Jimmy Cliff's 'I Can See Clearly Now'. It was more than a little surreal. When they ran out of material for the day, the channel synced up with the sepia-tinged broadcasts of *Cubavisión Internacional*, the international offshoot of Cuban state TV.

As propaganda it's pretty small-scale, low-impact stuff, although the range is about fifty kilometres, potentially reaching 60,000 viewers including Estepa, Écija and Osuna. They don't have any viewing figures for inside or outside the village, however. The station is often regarded with irritation in neighbouring villages for blocking other channels; on more than one occasion Spanish state prosecutors have begun legal proceedings because of the station's signal-squatting, piggy-backing on the frequencies owned by other, bigger stations, including, rumour has it, the Disney Channel.

There's an informational function to some of the output. The radio and TV stations are used to mobilise for upcoming demonstrations and land occupations, along with the union website, telephone chains, and neighbourly word-of-mouth. But for the most part, the content consists of trailers for life in the village, reminders of what 'we' stand for – which hits at that same issue of plurality in the village, or the lack of it. Paco Martos, the bright young guy I'd met on the coach to Malaga, one of the media hub's few full-time employees, was unapologetic about the fact they share a world-view with Marinaleda's Ayuntamiento: they may agree, but the significant thing is, he insisted, they don't take instruction from them.

There is, and has always been, one overwhelming problem for right-wing or liberal depictions of Marinaleda as a grotesque, demagogic dictatorship: Sánchez Gordillo keeps on winning elections. Again, and again, and again. He does so neither by slender, contestable margins, nor by margins so implausible that you'd be minded to send in UN election observers. As the crisis slowly saps all remaining credibility from the major parties, the rightist Popular Party (PP) and PSOE, Marinaleda is a jewel in the crown for IU, the coalition of left parties to which the CUT and Sánchez Gordillo belong.

Spanish local council elections are decided via a proportional share of the vote and use a party-list system, where you put your chosen party's piece of paper in an envelope, and that envelope in the ballot box: so the more votes IU receives, the more people on its list of candidates get elected. During the March 2012 local election, as the count proceeded in the Centro de Adultos, they would dramatically unfurl each anonymous ballot one by one, the Gordillistas in the room cheering each vote for IU. The mayor's supporters would dash out of the small classroom into the courtyard whenever IU had amassed enough votes for another councillor – 'We've got seven!' 'Now we've got eight!' – to huge cheers each time.

In a village where your political affinities (and their associated colour schemes, flags, heroes and icons) are held to be so important, election campaigns are periods of excitement, albeit rather one-sided excitement. The mayor's face appears on posters plastered all over the village, hanging from people's windows, and even strung as bunting across Avenida de la Libertad. It's a context in which the only real decision is whether to continue with Sánchez Gordillo, and the CUT/IU, and the project, or not – and if you choose the latter, you don't go around shouting about it. The old ladies of Marinaleda, some of the most loyal Gordillistas, have been known to approach newcomers to the village with a sweetly sincere explanation of how elections work, and have always worked: 'You will vote for *el alcalde*, won't you? You know you have to vote for *el alcalde*?'

Elections are free and ultimately fair, but in practice, they are a time to reaffirm commitment to the project. Sánchez Gordillo delivers lengthy orations from platforms about what they have achieved through struggle over the years, and what they will achieve next, and is re-elected comfortably. The glossy sixty-four-page 2011 CUT/IU election booklet, given to me when I first met Sánchez Gordillo in January 2012, and whipped out again by Rafa the librarian when I told him I was looking into the history of the village, is a first-class piece of propaganda, not least because it succeeds in the main aim of all Sánchez Gordillo arguments and propaganda: to conflate the idea of his project with the village as a whole, as one indistinguishable entity. Marinaleda *is* the project, rather than the village in which it has unfolded.

In those May 2011 elections, Sánchez Gordillo's CUT/ IU faced rumours the village might finally be slipping away to the PSOE – they had seen their vote fall from 71 per cent in 2003 to 61 per cent in 2007, and the PSOE claimed four of Marinaleda's eleven council seats. 'Alarm bells are ringing,' wrote one supporter of Sánchez Gordillo at the time. Perhaps the young people of the village were fed up with this archaic communist rhetoric? Perhaps the PSOE could exploit a burgeoning desire to move on from the mayor's obsession with working the land? The PSOE campaigned dirtily, using xenophobic populism, blaming illegal immigrants for the lack of work in Andalusia, and it failed spectacularly: CUT/IU won back their 9–2 majority on the council, winning 73 per cent.

The project was emphatically re-endorsed – and the celebrations that followed were appropriately Cuban. 'On election night, in the middle of the euphoria over the results,' wrote one blogger, '. . . it was decided by popular acclaim not to work the next day, and continue the celebrations with a great feast, of olives from the land, *salmorejo*, ham and cold beer.' This sounds like the end to every Asterix comic – the good side wins out, the village gathers as one, and the only thing missing is Cacofonix, tied to a tree. It's a pretty unusual response to an election result in the twenty-first century, though.

Until the mid 2000s, Marinaleda was surrounded by what was known as a *cinturón de hierro*, an 'iron belt' of PSOE control in the neighbouring towns of Estepa, Herrera, Écija and El Rubio. These villages were specially funnelled with investment from the Andalusian PSOE, who were determined to eradicate the embarrassing far-left anomaly in their midst. In this task they've failed, repeatedly – and yet, Marinaleda remains isolated. Beyond the boundaries of the *pueblo*, in the Sierra Sur region only Pedrera and Gilena maintain CUT majorities on their councils.

If it really is a utopia, argued one right-wing blogger, how come its principles have not been imported by nearby towns? 'Something must have failed in Marinaleda's heavenly oasis. Perhaps it's not an oasis after all, but an island disconnected from the rest of the world.' It's a fair point – it does raise questions that the people of neighbouring villages like El Rubio have never sought to emulate the experiment; but then every *pueblo* is composed of a unique tradition, personality and politics. It is not in the nature of

Andalusian *pueblos* to follow the same paths as one another; they are more likely to define themselves by their difference from their neighbours than seek to emulate them.

The most recent Andalusian regional elections, in March 2012, provide an interesting insight into the level of pluralism in the village: 1,199 people voted for Sánchez Gordillós IU, 331 for the PSOE, 222 for the PP, and 24 for others – which actually represented a small swing to IU from the PSOE since 2008. Clearly, there are at least 500 people in Marinaleda who vote against the left, against Sánchez Gordillo – and 200 of those vote for the conservative PP. You hear little of their views in the bars, or in the official narrative of the village's history – and yet, none of them have felt the need to flee for their own safety. Mostly they are the churchgoers, the smart dressers, probably with many friends among the *colectivistas*, the communists. They normally express their difference in the form of scepticism about their fellow villagers' relationship with Sánchez Gordillo: I have more than once encountered a tendency to explain away the success of his project with the argument that 'people are communist in name only, merely because they need work'.

In the assembly hall at the back of the Sindicato bar, the atmosphere is one of genuine democratic inclusion and participation. Maybe it's not as revolutionary as Sánchez Gordillo would have you believe, an inversion of the pyramid, an unprecedented novelty. After all, town hall meetings around the world, tenants' associations, even the parochialism of the Neighbourhood Watch, incorporate some of this kind of localist democracy: anyone with the time and interest can turn up, anyone with the confidence to do so can say anything, anyone can get angry without fear of reprisal. It's not solely Gordillistas who go to the general assemblies, although they are certainly a significant majority – not least because the discussion so often revolves around the development and management of El Humoso. PP or PSOE voters tend to dismiss it as a talking shop for members of the co-operative.

Attempts to reach out to the non-believers in nearby *pueblos* have not always gone well.

During the first of 2012's two nationwide general strikes in March, Sánchez Gordillo and the SAT went picketing in neighbouring towns – there would be, of course, little point picketing in Marinaleda itself, since no one would dream of working. During these general strikes, there were firm if invisible picket lines drawn everywhere: working in any context meant you supported Rajoy, the PP, austerity and the establishment. Five minutes down the road from Marinaleda, in El Rubio, the roaming picket discovered that the local secondary school had not been closed down. Only one pupil had shown up, but sixteen teachers were sitting in the staff room.

Sánchez Gordillo was in charge, directing what was theoretically an 'informational picket' with his megaphone. He was as ever standing at the front, saying clearly and repeatedly, 'Don't break the law, no fighting, no aggression', calling for persuasion rather than violence in the attempt to shut workplaces down. Meanwhile some of the young men, around thirty in total, jumped the fence at the rear of the school and allegedly proceeded to tour the building classroom by classroom, shouting and banging menacingly on the doors. Later that day, all sixteen teachers filed complaints with the local Guardia Civil in Herrera, and cases are still pending against some SAT members. That same day there were accusations of aggressive picketing, scaring primary-school children in El Rubio, and thefts by those on strike totalling €500 during 'forced closures' of some businesses. A couple of times the Guardia were called, but by then the culprits had disappeared.

'It was impossible to say whether Sánchez Gordillo quietly approved, with a nod and a wink, of what was going on,' one of Marinaleda's English residents told me. 'Because he kept saying quite clearly, "Don't break the law, no fighting" – but he was still kind of in charge.' In one of the businesses they occupied, in Casariche, he'd been using his megaphone to say: 'Have a coffee, but pay for it if you do.' It's a delicate ambiguity for him to maintain – though in the eyes of the Spanish press, and presumably the Guardia, Sánchez Gordillo's culpability was pretty clear. They relished connecting him to the painting of FASCISTA in big letters on the car of a strike-breaking teacher in another nearby village, Badolatosa.

On every demonstration, on every picket, Sánchez

Gordillo is always there with the megaphone. He is the human megaphone for the concerns of his people, and he is loved and hated for it in equal measure. The kind of forays into nearby *pueblos* they carried out during the general strike of March 2012 cut to the heart of why there's genuine contempt towards Marinaleda from some of its neighbours. Another English *marinaleña*, Ali, recalls being practically assaulted by a random stranger in a supermarket in Écija, once she found out she'd come from Marinaleda. 'How can you live there?!' the woman had shouted. 'Don't you know they are communists?!' Perhaps significantly, when it left the PSOE 'iron belt' in 2011, Écija became a PP town.

Of course, that immediate identification of an individual with their *pueblo*, however historically ingrained in Andalusian culture, does not give an accurate picture of any place. There are PP voters in Marinaleda. There are certainly communists in Écija, for that matter. As we saw in the previous chapter with regard to religious observation and practice in Marinaleda, the story rehashed to visiting journalists by Sánchez Gordillo omits plenty. No *pueblo* can ever be entirely united or consistent.

When you're living in an oasis, or a communist theme park, or any small village, really, it can get claustrophobic – and it's always beneficial to get out for a while, for a bit of perspective. Back up on the balcony of Andalusia, in

Estepa, I was glad to have a day or two to breathe the colder, drier air and let the oxygen go to work, processing utopia with the help of the salty local sherries.

Among the *estepeños* I found a general sense of pride in their local curiosity down in the valley, but this pride was often tinged with scepticism. There is, some older *estepeños* thought, a gap between the village's ideal and its reality. 'The mayor is not perfect,' they kept saying; 'it is not perfect.' One portly, well-read businessman in comfortable middle age, with a warm, solid handshake, was especially keen to talk to me (anonymously) about Marinaleda. He was amused and gratified that I had come such a long way to visit the Sierra Sur, and regarded Sánchez Gordillo with heavily caveated admiration – but admiration nonetheless. He showed me Félix Talego's book, which, like several local history buffs I'd met, he had tracked down despite it being an obscure academic tome unknown even to ruthlessly thorough websites like Amazon.

'*Si la trabajas con tus manos y la riegas con tu sudor, tuya es la tierra, trabajador*', he recited, dusting off a part of his encyclopaedic brain and quoting Sánchez Gordillo's 1980 book. The phrase translates somewhat less poetically as 'If you work it with your hands and water it with your sweat, the land is yours, worker' – but it is the Marinaleda philosophy encapsulated. After Franco's death, the businessman told me, the Spanish people felt lost, suddenly deprived of a patriarch. It was a scary, fractious time, and while most of

Spain 'ran around like a headless chicken', Sánchez Gordillo captivated the working class with declamations like the one above. That makes him sound a bit like a cynical opportunist, I said – is that how you see him? 'No, don't misunderstand me, I think the town is based on noble, wonderful ideals. But the reality is not so perfect.'

Isn't it a bit unreasonable to expect it to be perfect? Absolutely, he said, they shouldn't be attacked for imperfection; things are hardly perfect in Estepa, either. 'It's just that you shouldn't believe everything Sánchez Gordillo says. When someone quarrels with him, it becomes difficult for that person to continue to live in Marinaleda.' There are of course no gulags, no Stasi-style holding cells, no show trials, but it becomes 'difficult' to live there. People gossip, he explained, and make your life hard in petty little ways. Perhaps that's actually a small-town difficulty, rather than an ideological one? In *pueblos* of that size, when people talk, everyone talks. Sure, he said: ostracism and gossip are more of a danger than anything else – they are the only danger, in fact.

I heard the same innuendoes a few times from *estepeños*, that opposing the mayor can lead to 'problems'. One whom I met had more than just innuendo and insinuations – she had a tip-off about two Marinaleda 'exiles' living in Estepa. I took some details, made some phone calls, and eventually Javi helped me find the address of this allegedly dissident man and his wife. On a deathly quiet residential street in mid-afternoon, cobbles tumbling down the valley beneath us, we rang the doorbell, and a woman answered. She greeted us warmly – oh, an Englishman! – but when we explained our purpose, and mentioned the M-word, she retreated into the doorway a little.

Careless talk doesn't cost lives out here, but it can cost friendships. In the name of prudence, I stood at a distance, as Javi made earnest assurances that we would maintain her and her husband's anonymity, that I could be trusted. 'I'll take your number in case my husband is willing to speak to you when he gets in,' she said, with a look that seemed to add: 'and he definitely, definitely won't.'

As we walked away from the house, Javi tried to account for this reluctance to speak. There is an expression in Spain, he told me, *'no querer remover la mierda'*; you don't want to stir up the shit, because it smells worse. You let the bad things in your past lie dormant. It's a phrase which sums up a lot about a nation which has spent three decades under theoretical observance of an official 'pact of forgetting' about their civil war and fascist dictatorship. Now, at last, some of the mass graves of those killed by Franco are being dug up, and the remains given proper burials. In left-wing communities like Marinaleda, they haven't forgotten so easily: one programme on the radio station is called *Without Memory, There Is no History*.

There is of course no equivalence here, between a Spanish elite that connived in covering up the mass murder and torture of Franco's White Terror, and a village mayor who has simplified the narrative of his people's struggle a little, and perhaps overlooked the odd act of intimidation carried out by comrades. But while the Gordillistas rightly chide the nation around it for shrinking away from awkward questions about recent Spanish history, it's a shame that some of the village's own imperfections are brushed under the carpet.

Unsurprisingly, the exile never called me back.

7

The Village Against the Crisis

March 2013: driving west along the Andalusian coast road, from Malaga towards Jerez, the deep, layered, tree-lined hills facing the sea are disfigured by the marks of what the locals call the 'brick crisis'. For once, the Costa del Sol looks like it's never seen the *sol* in its life: swathed in dense fog, and the kind of rain that is so light yet so all-pervasive you're not sure if it's mist, precipitation, or sea-spray. Under portentous slate-grey skies, the hills have an almost mystical aspect. Here and there, concrete construction frames are cut arbitrarily into the rock. Some of these housing projects are barely started, just Meccano frames, steel girders slowly breaking out in rust. There are others which are further along the construction process: whole rows of houses, painted, rooved, but still without windows. Some are finished, and empty.

It's as if the wind changed suddenly, and the new weather front froze everything where it stood. The numbers are unsurprisingly hard to pin down, but respectable estimates put the number of vacant properties in Spain at 4 million, of which 900,000 are new-builds. Altogether, 16 per cent of the country's entire housing stock is empty. A staggering 400,000 families have been evicted by their mortgage lenders since the crash, over 20,000 people are on the streets (double the number in 2008), and uncountable numbers are now squatting. Some Spanish estate agents have been reluctant to put up 'For Sale' signs on vacant properties, for fear that doing so will attract squatters.

When you've grown up somewhere as cluttered and crowded as London, with its green belt tied tight around a swollen waistline, it's difficult to conceive just how much vacant space there is for building in Spain. The country's land mass is twice the size of the UK, with a smaller population. There's space everywhere. So they built, everywhere.

The unsustainable fetish for growth that created the crisis was – like everything else in Spain – a physical act. Where the rest of Europe would content itself with a metaphor, Spain just had to be literal: it built its prosperity on unsure foundations, never thinking about the future. And now there's no money to finish the job, only stagnation and decay. Everyone I've met across Andalusia in the last few years knows people who've lost jobs in the construction industry, not to mention the related professions that suffered the knock-on effects – glaziers, roofers, clerks, surveyors, and of course, the vital business of housing, feeding and cosseting expatriates and tourists. Spain's empty patios now echo, hollow. In the space which traditionally hosted the sociable tumult of Spanish family life, there are only dried-up fountains, the stillness of a nation's enforced inertia.

These ruins of late capitalism scar the Spanish landscape. Spain has long had a grimly fascinating number of ghost towns: from the Civil War, when villagers fled for their lives, never to return, and from the 1950s and 1960s, when people escaped rural poverty in search of work. While Marinaleda's population declined by 30 per cent during the 1960s for this reason, some small hamlets were abandoned altogether, and never repopulated.

The trend for dramatic, mesmerising photographs of Detroit's burned-out factories and abandoned homes has coined the term 'ruin porn'. The Spanish equivalent is speculation porn, exemplified by photo-spreads in the newspapers of entire new Madrid suburbs built on the assumption of relentless growth and completed just before the crash. These modern ghost towns are haunted by a different mortal terror to Detroit's: not the decay of previously thriving communities, but the folly of baseless expansion, of urban spaces that have never been used and may never be used. An architect's impression, a blueprint of blind optimism, sketched out in three dimensions and now abandoned: rust sleeping on the gates, tumbleweed in the gardens, lamps illuminating empty streets, brand new street signs pointing nowhere. Permanent vacancy.

Over the last few years *la crisis* in Spain – that distant land, beyond the borders of the village – has become a permanent state of affairs; it is a phrase you hear so often in news reports and everyday conversations, it almost loses meaning. *La crisis* is not a moment, not even an unpleasantly long-lasting event, but the state of things.

In May and June 2011, as the PSOE government stuttered towards its inevitable collapse, and unemployment, foreclosures and debt soared to astounding new highs, the Spanish people mounted their first serious response to the crisis. The now famous *indignados* movement began in Madrid with the occupation of the capital's iconic central square, the Puerta del Sol, on 15 May 2011, and over the following weeks spread out into all of Spain's major towns and cities, until it was a truly national phenomenon, identified by the name 15-M or 'the Spanish revolution'. The broadest phrasing of the many demands emanating from the 15-M encampments was for 'real democracy now'. Its pluralistic anti-capitalism, horizontalism, pacifism, general assemblies and working groups became both the template and the immediate inspiration for the global Occupy movement, in America and beyond. A study for Ipsos Public Affairs that summer found between 6 and 8.5 million people, in a country of only 48 million, said they had taken part: 76 per cent of those polled said their demands were reasonable, and only 7 per cent were opposed to the protests.

'We are', announced one especially totemic 15-M

slogan, 'neither right nor left: we are coming from the bottom and we're going for the top.'

Seville may be a city of historic renown, a major international tourist destination, and the capital of Andalusia, but it's not actually very big: it's less than a quarter of the size of Madrid. Nonetheless, the day protests exploded into life there, 29 May 2011, over 30,000 people spilled out of the Metro and into the Plaza de España. The Plaza was the central exhibit in the 1929 Sevilla Expo, a massive monument from a world fair built on the brink of global collapse, a space so wide and open it makes you catch your breath – with only the central fountain to draw your eye away from the sumptuous tiles of the perimeter; it hosts the best kind of emptiness, a vacancy that demands to be filled with people. And then, drums playing, in the glorious heat of early summer, they marched past the world's largest cathedral, past the Moorish Giralda tower, past Plaza Nueva, where the city hall is, and eventually halted on the newly finished public-private architectural monstrosity widely known as The Mushroom. The camp lasted a month there, with thousands sleeping over for some or all of the period, yearning for the full experience, the corporeal solidarity.

Amid Seville's wizened stone and garlanded history, the demand was for something new. If they were to start creating 'real democracy now', as their slogan demanded, it would be focused on horizontal organisation, mass assemblies, and consensus-based decision making. A resurgent sincerity seemed to emerge from the swamp of postmodernist irony, just as it did in New York. In both cases, they meant business. 'They wanted to take it seriously,' Emma the *indignada* told me, when I met her later that year. 'Drinking was forbidden, because it was not supposed to just become a party, so at one or two in the morning people were just chatting quietly about politics, or sleeping. A lot of different topics came up, with people who wanted to help Palestine or the Sahara. You had a schedule, day by day, a lot of events and discussions. People were bringing food from home to The Mushroom – there were people from nearby villages and towns outside Seville, including Marinaleda.'

Emma was not an experienced activist, and she seemed particularly eager that I understand her consternation at just how broad and unprecedented a movement it was: 15-M was something unique and special, the source of an empowering head-rush of new possibilities. This, she explained, was a new level of participation, involving more than just the usual suspects such as the leftist parties, anarchists, *perroflautas* (hippies) and socialist trade unions.

'Of course,' Emma continued, 'there was a big representation from Marinaleda at 15-M, they hired a big bus so everybody could come to Seville. Marinaleda is really, really important for us.' Why is that, I asked? 'Because here we are really too quiet, and they are not. I'm so excited you're going there,' she said, kindly, like I was in for a treat.

'Before I went to Marinaleda, I had this idea of it being a very revolutionary place, and it is, but . . . it's really the old people who are like that. The young people you see there don't seem to be conscious of how lucky they are, of all the things they have. It's really weird. They live in a kind of bubble, they don't realise what the world is like elsewhere.'

So they don't ever leave the bubble?

'Well, I've never met anyone from Marinaleda who is not actually living there. You're not going to find a really intellectual place there – don't misunderstand me, it's people who've been working all their lives, but before, they were working for big landowners.'

For centuries, there has been anger across the south of Spain about the *latifundios*. 'But in Marinaleda,' she said emphatically, '– in Marinaleda they didn't get angry, they just went! They broke down the gate, got inside, knocked on the door and said "We need land".' Her admiration for the *marinaleños* as people who act out their class war, rather than merely talking about it, as pseudo-intellectual city folk are wont to do, was not in the least patronising – there was genuine longing in her voice, for that level of political integrity. The dedication to direct action certainly tallies with the history of the Andalusian *pueblos*. Sánchez Gordillo would later cite to me the notion of 'propaganda of the deed' as anarchism's greatest influence on his politics.

The 15-M participants not only protested against the dire state the crisis had left them in, they also announced their complete lack of faith in the established parliamentary parties – in parliamentary politics at all – to solve any of these problems. It was thus inevitable when, in November 2011's general election, plagued by incompetence and incumbency, the nominally centre-left PSOE were ousted in favour of the rightist PP. The left-wing coalition IU, which Sánchez Gordillo's CUT party belongs to, doubled their previous vote share to 7 per cent nationally, but to expect the *indignados*' energy and numbers to be transformed into any kind of game-changing protest vote is to misunderstand the nature of their indignation.

Most of the *indignados* had abstained, the PSOE vote tumbled from 44 to 29 per cent, and the remaining rump of voters elected Mariano Rajoy as the first PP prime minister since 2004. There are, a 15-M member called Juanjo told me at the time, 10 million Spaniards who will always vote PP, whatever happens – so if everyone else opts out, they're going to win.

The 15-M movement had informed not just Spain, but the world, that millions of Spaniards were unwilling to brook the crisis. They were desperately looking for an alternative to the current system – and yet, in their midst, there was already one in operation. They may have ignored it before, or dismissed it with a chuckle as a rural curiosity run by a bearded eccentric; but they could do so no longer. 'What are your demands? What is your alternative?' barked the dogs of capitalist realism. And, especially in the south, the *indignados* were able to respond: 'Well, how about Marinaleda?'

It seems almost too obvious to say, but Marinaleda is a village of fewer than 3,000 people. It is not a political party, it is not a revolutionary national movement, and it is not an ideology in itself. Its ability to provide an answer to all of Spain's problems was, and is, clearly limited.

And yet the *marinaleños* used the small bully pulpit that 15-M afforded them with gusto. Throughout 2011, Sánchez Gordillo took every opportunity to get the message across on TV, in the press, and in the Andalusian parliament that the Spanish people were being unduly punished for capitalism's crisis, and it was time to resist, as the village had done.

Then, at the end of 2011, came Marinaleda's latest highly public contretemps with the Spanish nobility. This time it extended beyond the Duchess of Alba, to her son – and on this occasion it was definitely the noble who started it. Cayetano Luis Martínez de Irujo y Fitz-James Stuart, also known as the Olympic horse-riding Duke of Salvatierra, made some blithely provocative public remarks which enraged the *marinaleños*. First, Cayetano said he agreed with a right-wing Catalan nationalist politician that Andalusian workers were using government subsidies to get drunk, sponging off the richer Catalans. Shortly afterwards, he was challenged about this in a TV interview. Surely, the interviewer said, the sharp rise in poverty in the south was due to the crisis, not to the fecklessness of the workers? Cayetano responded that Andalusia was 'a fraud', where no one wanted to work and backwardness was ingrained: 'When you see these young people, who have absolutely no desire whatsoever to progress, that's serious. That only happens in Andalusia.'

In a sense, this kind of casual upper-class prejudice is so predictable it might just have been ignored; you suspect a similar outrage in the UK might have provoked a few muttered swear words and some rolled eyes. In Marinaleda they opted for a slightly more robust, direct response: they occupied Cayetano's land.

'He owns fourteen *cortijos* between Cordoba and Seville, and the Duchess of Alba has 35,000 hectares,' Sánchez Gordillo told me the following month. For Cayetano to have the gall to complain about Andalusian labourers living off farm subsidies was, like the House of Alba itself, pretty ridiculously rich. 'They receive so much help!' laughed Sánchez Gordillo. 'Together with the Queen of England, the *duquesa* is the one who receives the most money from the PAC [Common Agricultural Policy]: she receives €3 million a year. So we occupied the *cortijos* and said he had to retract his comments.'

Camped out on his lands, they had ample opportunity to explain the huge disparity in Andalusian land ownership, and EU subsidies, to visiting members of the press eager for a quirky angle on *la crisis*. Sánchez Gordillo and his fellow occupiers made another demand: that Cayetano cease hiring illegal workers through private contractors who operate 'like the mafia', brutalising the illegal workers and native *jornaleros* alike.

Not for the first time, the village won. In the subsequent PR climbdown, Cayetano accepted all their demands, apologised, and travelled to the south to meet Sánchez Gordillo and see Marinaleda for himself. It was a humbling experience for the young nobleman, who publicly professed his gratitude for an 'enriching' day visiting El Humoso and seeing all the work going on there. 'Sometimes we think things are one way, and then realise they are very different,' he admitted to *El Público*.

Spain's film crews and journalists were once again zeroing in on Marinaleda, waiting patiently for Sánchez Gordillo's next outburst, or the next piece of direct action from the *Sindicato Andaluz de Trabajadores* (SAT). When the crisis started sinking Spain, it raised up the one existing alternative in its midst, throwing the village's exceptional past and unique present into sharper relief than ever. The *indignados* were more than a protest movement, they had declared their desire for a different way of living; and so, despite its awkward size and location, Marinaleda was the obvious choice for an Andalusian-wide 15-M reunion rally in November 2011.

Sánchez Gordillo described this event as a kind of Andalusian awakening: it was video-streamed from their town hall to tens of thousands, and hundreds of visitors came for the occasion. When he addressed the meeting, he spoke, at breakneck speed as usual, about dreams and injustices, and the urgent need to mend the gap between the utopian ideal and the grim reality. He finished his speech by quoting Che's words: 'Only those who dream will someday see their dreams converted to reality.' He added that it was not enough to believe in a different world – it was time to have the courage to live as if it had already arrived.

Other speakers at the rally included spokespeople from a new anti-capitalist co-operative in Valencia, and Enric Duran, an infamous young Catalan who borrowed €492,000 from thirty-nine different financial institutions, with no intention of paying it back, and distributed it among a variety of different co-operatives and revolutionary projects. If Marinaleda is Asterix's village, pluckily holding out against the Romans despite the enormous odds stacked against them, then 15-M was like a simultaneous discovery, across the vast reaches of the empire, that maybe everyone else had access to the magic potion, too.

When I interviewed Sánchez Gordillo that winter, he was, as usual, entirely confident in his world-view and the stark contrast between what they were creating and the world outside. To his credit, there was not a sliver of triumphalism in his analysis; it was stern, and sober.

'The myth of capitalism has crumbled,' he announced, 'that the market is an omnipotent God that fixes everything with his invisible hand. We've seen this is a great lie, a stupid fundamentalism: we've seen that in times of crisis, markets have had to resort to the state, and that states are putting money into the banks.'

And so they were – hundreds of billions of euros' worth. In Spain, 75 per cent of debt is private. There was no extravagant public spending that created the crisis there; in 2008 Spain's finances were well within the Eurozone's fiscal rules, and its government debt as a share of GDP was much lower than Germany's, a situation they maintained, to begin with. In Spain, essentially, it is the crash which created the debt, not the other way around.

'If there were any justice in the world the big bankers, and the governments that allowed them to perpetrate their economic terrorism, would be in jail. And those same people who caused the crisis are the ones who now want to fix it. The pyromaniac wants to play the fireman! Mrs Merkel and Mr Sarkozy want to speak for the banks and fix what they caused.

'Everywhere there's crisis: an agricultural crisis, an industrial crisis, a financial crisis, a food crisis, a *system* crisis. Before, people had work, so they didn't think twice about it. Here in Andalusia there was a boom in construction, and things were getting built everywhere. A construction worker would earn three, four or five thousand euros per month – a lot of money! Then when we lost those jobs, people began losing their homes, because they couldn't pay the mortgage, so the banks have been repossessing them. And so now people are seeking refuge in agriculture instead, and in other formulas that aren't those of capitalism.' And how serious are those formulas? Sánchez Gordillo rejected the idea that 15-M was 'merely reformist', as some of its leftist critics have contended: it was developing, he said, 'an increasingly anti-capitalist vision'.

In London, I told him, big-state social democracy on the post-war model was increasingly seen as finished. The centre-left approach, of a compromise with capitalism, was kaput: apart from anything else, if someone won't meet you halfway, it's not a compromise anymore. Just like 15-M, the people at Occupy London and Occupy Wall Street were looking for alternative models wherever they could find them, however obscure the location. In fact, I explained, that's kind of what brought me here. He nodded sympathetically.

'People no longer care if it's this party or another party, PP or PSOE; they want to change the system to one that isn't capitalistic, with unions, parties and organisations that promote a different system, with human beings at the core. People are considered merchandise: while they're profitable, they're used, and when they're no longer profitable, they're discarded. We have to change these cruel and inhuman values. I have dedicated my entire life to this.'

He wrote 'PP' and 'PSOE' on the scrap paper in front of him, drew a circle around each, then one bigger circle around the outside. Stabbing the edge of this impromptu Venn diagram with the point of the pencil, he said simply: 'It's *all* capitalism.'

A few months later, Sánchez Gordillo had his contempt for 'the capitalist parties' and his sense of realpolitik tested, when he was unexpectedly given the chance to take some small parliamentary advantage of the crisis. Following the general election at the end of 2011, March 2012 saw elections to the regional parliament in Seville: the PP were the largest party by a sliver but did not win a majority, and the prospect of a PSOE–IU coalition emerged. During the weeks of coalition talks, Sánchez Gordillo was being widely mentioned as a possible minister in a hypothetical PSOE–IU government – something which would have required him to abandon the mayoralty, and abandon Marinaleda both politically and geographically. He had been a deputy while still living in the village, but he couldn't be a minister and not move to Seville.

A compromise with the PSOE would have brought Sánchez Gordillo a great deal more power and influence, a bigger bully pulpit, and a voice in policy-making across Andalusia. Instead, he launched a revolt.

The PSOE, he announced, were a party without principle – and if they went into coalition with this 'capitalist' party, IU would be, too. 'We cannot bring ourselves closer to the sinking ship', Sánchez Gordillo told *El Mundo*, and warned in the strongest possible language that such a coalition would mean legitimising the PSOE and ushering in austerity-lite, while sending the left 'to hell' as a stooge of the capitalist parties. As it happened, IU split in two, the party leadership made a pact with the PSOE, and Sánchez Gordillo's warnings about more austerity and cuts were almost immediately vindicated. It was an articulation of another of his maxims: if you can't win the fight, at least keep faith with your principles.

The first time we met, I'd noticed how his gesticulations grew increasingly theatrical and effusive, and his trilled rrrr's ever faster, ever raspier, the bigger the issues and ideas became. He was quite capable of working himself up into a revolutionary tumult, never mind anyone else. At the time I wondered if he was being wasted on such a small stage, as the mayor of a village of 2,700 people. What with his long-proven penchant for headline-grabbing actions, not to mention the three-hour declamations on Marinaleda TV, I wondered whether he, too, hankered for a bigger platform. Whether he wanted it or not, by August 2012, he would have it.

Marinaleda had already proven, as far back as 1980, that the month of August was optimal for seizing the national media narrative in the name of the people. In 2012, they repeated the performance. With members of SAT from other villages – including Sánchez Gordillo's partner in crime, the union's national spokesman, Diego Cañamero – they occupied land belonging to the Ministry of Defence, a farm called Las Turquillas. This was, they argued, land in the public domain that did not serve the public. Over 200 *jornaleros* camped out for eighteen days, until violently evicted by the Guardia, and used the media attention to call for the land to be cultivated and given over to the unemployed.

It was the first time they had united their prelapsarian belief, that 'the land belongs to those who work it', with the new misery of the financial crisis. They were occupying, Sánchez Gordillo told *El Mundo*, on behalf of '6 million unemployed, 12 million poor people, 1.7 million families with all members unemployed, and 30 per cent of Andalusian families living below the poverty line'. The land's sole purpose, he explained, was to accrue EU subsidies for the Ministry of Defence, like the *latifundios* belonging to the aristocrats of the House of Alba and Infantado. Neither sets of subsidies were putting any bread on the tables of Andalusian *jornaleros*.

While the land was occupied, tents erected, and cooking rotas put into practice, and they had the press's attention, SAT moved onto the next stage of their plan. It was to be an ingenious escalation.

Their targets were two major chain-store supermarkets in Andalusia, one a Carrefour in Arcos de la Frontera, near Cadiz, the other a branch of Mercadona in Écija, down the road from Marinaleda. Several hundred SAT activists showed up at each of the two supermarkets, and while the majority rallied outside, a small group went in, filled ten or so carts with basic foodstuffs – oil, sugar, chickpeas, rice, pasta, milk, biscuits and vegetables – and left without paying. There were some scuffles with a few of the supermarket employees, but in both cases, they emerged with the 'expropriated' goods to cheers from the rest of the crowd. The food was then donated to the *Corrala Utopía* in Seville, a series of apartment blocks occupied (with the help of the local 15-M) by homeless families evicted by their banks, and to civic centres in Cadiz, where it would be passed on to the unemployed. The message was impossible to misread: under capitalism – under *la crisis* – major supermarket chains make hundreds of millions of euros in profit for their shareholders from selling food, while hundreds of thousands around them go hungry.

It was both spontaneous and shocking, a deliberate and ostentatious act of Robin Hood–style redistribution; and yet it was well planned enough that they had a professional agency photographer and film crew inside the supermarkets with them, to get footage of the SAT activists loading up the trolleys. These photos, and pictures of Sánchez Gordillo declaiming on his megaphone outside Mercadona, swept the story onto the Spanish front pages, to the top slot in the evening news, and, via Reuters and the international news wires, across the world – not only in Europe and America, but India, Iran, Australia and China. 'We want to expropriate the expropriators,' Sánchez Gordillo declared. 'By that we mean the landlords, banks and big supermarkets, which are making money from the economic crisis.'

The Spanish establishment panicked. The raids were immediately and aggressively condemned by the PP and the PSOE as wanton, despicable criminality – perpetrated by an elected member of the Andalusian parliament, no less. Even the IU leadership distanced itself from Sánchez Gordillo. José Antonio Griñán, the leader of the PSOE– IU coalition in the Andalusian parliament, called it 'barbarism'. And yet, the Spanish right struggled to turn the popular mood against Sánchez Gordillo: whether you agreed with the stunt or not, the crisis was so widespread, as was dismay over its uneven effects on the poor, that even cynics understood the point. Popular sympathy seemed to be on their side. Fifty-four per cent of those polled by *El Mundo*, not a left-leaning newspaper by any stretch, supported the action.

Sánchez Gordillo's success in spinning the raids was in part thanks to his refusal to self-aggrandise and blow them out of proportion. He did not pretend for a minute that expropriating ten trolleys' worth of rice and chickpeas was an act of redistribution big enough to change any lives: yes, it was a stunt – but it was a vital one. The raids were, in fact, 'propaganda of the deed', as he explained to the media: 'We are obliged to grab attention in this way so that somebody stops and thinks. They have to understand that people here are desperate.'

Press and TV demand grew throughout August, and the supermarket raids were the media's main talking point for weeks: news programmes visited Andalusian food banks and soup kitchens, discussed rising food prices, foreclosures, and the impossibility of getting work. When he had finished all of his national (and international) TV spots, Sánchez Gordillo used the brouhaha to announce a three-week march across the Spanish south, in the middle of a devastating August heat wave, to highlight the crisis. The plan was to call upon his fellow small-town mayors along the way and try to persuade them to default on their debt repayments. The rural *pueblos* did not cause the crisis and should not be made to pay for them, he explained; it was an attempt to link up some of the chain of separate communities, to build solidarity. Little came of the march, ostensibly, but it kept the issues – and their iconic advocate, with the grey beard and the keffiyeh – in the headlines for an extra fortnight.

As the dust settled on Marinaleda's month of notoriety, it became easier to see the expropriations as part of a wider pattern of behaviour. They were a spectacular addition to a growing armoury of acts of everyday anti-capitalist resistance, new (and not so new) coping behaviours brought on by necessity, in the face of the crisis. Barcelona-based sociologist Carlos Delclós identified the supermarket raids as a 'public policy correction', whereby the crisis of legitimacy at the heart of Spanish democracy, at the heart of capitalism, demanded a pro-active intervention from its subjects. 'We should never forget that democracy means "people power,"' he wrote, 'and that correcting a lack of democracy means exercising power from the bottom up, occupying the cracks in the architecture of repression, and breaking it open like rhizomic roots shattering concrete.'

Thousands of microcosmic acts of quotidian resistance were already taking place, Delclós observed: 'citizens refusing to pay outrageous fees for public transportation and toll roads, doctors refusing to deny free health care to undocumented immigrants, and police refusing orders to assault protesters – while people all over the country are referring to taking a Robin Hood stance on shoplifting as "pulling a Gordillo" (via the hashtag #HazteUnGordillo)'. To this we can add the firefighters and locksmiths across Spain who have refused to evict families foreclosed by their banks, and even the widely recognised explosion in *dinero negro*, the black market; cash-in-hand work has ballooned since the crisis.

Of course, poverty in Spain was not invented by the crisis – even in the heyday of the economic miracle, there were people living on the streets and families struggling to feed their children. The crash catalysed an explosion of that misery across parts of the Spanish class system which had never before experienced it. According to a 2013 report by the FOESSA Foundation looking into social exclusion and the crisis, 380,000 Spanish households had been without a single employed member before the crisis: by the end of 2012 this number had more than quadrupled, to 1.8 million. The numbers continue to horrify, but they do so in the abstract. The great significance of Sánchez Gordillo's latest intervention was that it highlighted what no one else in power would dare: 'that the crisis has first and last names, faces and ID cards'.

I never encountered *Schadenfreude* in Marinaleda directed at the architects of the collapse, much less, of course, at its victims. The response of the villagers, like that of Sánchez Gordillo himself, was sombre and pessimistic: this is what capitalism does, this is what any kind of centralised power does. The Spanish people, who have suffered so much in the past, even the relatively recent past, are now condemned to suffer again. One 15-M activist in Seville told me that one of the main reasons there had not already been a revolution was cultural: Spaniards were stoically resigned to the fact that their earthly life would be a 'valley of tears'. And like the good Catholics they were, they would endure the pain.

By 2011, *marinaleños* were seeing the effects on their friends and relatives in neighbouring *pueblos* and farther afield: the girlfriend in Casariche whose business had folded; the friends in Estepa who could only get odd jobs, or a couple of months of seasonal work in the *mantecados* factories; the cousins in Valencia facing eviction from their home.

By 2013, they were starting to notice the effects inside the village, too. In among my scrawled notes from the Marinaleda February *carnaval*, the pages in my notebook swollen by beer stains and dusted with loose threads of rolling tobacco, I found one sentence that stood out, underlined three times, from a middle-aged local called Pepe: 'It's a bad time for Marinaleda – but it might be a good time for the revolution.'

8

The End of Utopia?

In retrospect, things got a bit out of hand in August 2012. The supermarket expropriations and ensuing media mayhem, as well as the surrounding three-week march and land occupations, catapulted Sánchez Gordillo into the public eye. He was a major problem for Rajoy's government and their allies – even for their parliamentary enemies in the PSOE – because he made it clear the crisis was not an unavoidable act of God, but a consequence of their economic and political system. Therefore it was something that could be contested, perhaps even defeated. With the Robin Hood mayor in the spotlight, more and more people were talking about Marinaleda, and what it stood for.

While the message that propelled him there had been deadly serious, the danger is, when you reach a certain level of recognition in contemporary pop culture, that the message can be obscured by the spectacle. His fame reached its first peak of bathos in September that year, when the global youth clothing chain H&M created a Sánchez

Gordillo t-shirt. Appropriately, the design was part of their new 'Zeitgeist' collection, and showed a hand grasping an ear of maize, accompanied by the words 'Food to the people! No world hunger' – Juan Manuel Sánchez Gordillo'. H&M withdrew the design within four days, issuing an official apology that they hadn't intended 'to take sides' and were 'sorry if any customers have felt offended'. It was a sign of how charged the supermarket raids were, in the context of capitalism's crisis, that a message like 'food to the people' might be deemed contro-versial, or even offensive.

In the winter that followed, Sánchez Gordillo was to receive the ultimate accolade in Andalusian pop culture: he was honoured in a *chirigota* – a unique, phenomenally popular form of satirical folk song, emanating from the province of Cadiz. Traditionally, *chirigota* groups comprise around ten to fifteen people, who sing chorally in the streets and squares, in costume, performing a repertoire of self-composed songs about the state of the nation, the government, or society; sometimes pruriently, always laced with wit. Suppressed by Franco, they have made a huge comeback in recent decades, and the annual knock-out competition for best *chirigota* group, as part of the Lenten carnival in Cadiz, has become a national cultural and TV event.

But Sánchez Gordillo wasn't just the subject of a satiri-cal song, as politicians often are – he was the model for a group's entire repertoire: Los Gordillos, they called themselves. Every detail of their outfits was based on how he had looked in the news reports the previous August: twelve adult men dressed in white shorts, red check shirts, green keffiyehs, sun hats and desert boots, wearing bushy grey beards, and incorporating props like supermarket trolleys, Andalusian flags, and loud-hailers into their performance. They were one of the hits of the 2013 *carnaval*, reaching the quarter-final of the official competition and winning the hearts of many aficionados with songs about the supermarket raids performed in front of a giant Mercadona backdrop.

While his notoriety was skyrocketing and the media requests continued to flood in, the day-to-day operations of the village were not disturbed by this Sánchez Gordillo mania – Marinaleda was robust enough to withstand controversies over t-shirt slogans and irreverent comedy songs. They had endured worse. But the economic crisis was starting to have an impact on the village in less visible ways.

Two weeks after Spain's second general strike of the year, on 30 November 2012, a three-day 'march of the women' from Marinaleda to Seville was due to arrive in the city's historic Plaza de España for a rally, and to seek an audience with the regional government to discuss the crisis and its effect on farming communities. It was an expression of the sporadic feminist orientation of the village's politics. 'Everything we have won here, has been thanks to the women', Sánchez Gordillo once told me, and although some aspects of Spain's old-fashioned gender roles persist (especially when it comes to housework), women are over-represented on the village council and in general assemblies.

The square was almost deserted at midday on a Thursday out of season, with just a few tourists inspecting the mosaics and an ice-cream seller in a daydream, untroubled by custom. Into this tranquillity arrived SAT and the *marinaleños*: a couple of hundred marchers, most of them women, accompanied by two large, slow-crawling vans with numerous speakers strapped to their rooves. Chants about revolution and the bankers rang out into the empty plaza as they parked up outside the Andalusian regional government offices.

Their march over, packed lunches were distributed: mortadella sandwiches wrapped in tinfoil and cartons of orange juice. A local TV news crew and a couple of regional newspapers arrived. There were a lot of keffiyehs, a lot of SAT flags, a lot of sensible walking clothes, and smiles all round – ordinary people who are used to struggle as a way of life. A woman wheeled a buggy past me, and it took me a moment to notice it was being used to transport a bundle of Andalusian flags. When you routinely go on three-day marches to make a point about farm subsidies, it's fair to say it comes with a uniquely intense attitude to political engagement, to the way politics sits in your everyday life.

The speeches began, and Diego Cañamero proceeded to explain – in as fiery manner as is possible, given the subject matter – why it was necessary to abolish the *peonadas*, the daily record-keeping system by which *jornaleros* receive social security payments. 'We must eliminate the rural employment plan, and eliminate capitalism,' he continued. With his SAT t-shirt and jeans, cropped silver hair, and reddish-brown skin, clean-shaven and weathered like old leather, he always makes a good partner to Sánchez Gordillo.

I hadn't noticed *el alcalde* at first: he did not seem to be one of the four speakers on the podium, and I thought perhaps he had skipped a march for once. Then I spotted him deep in the crowd, about halfway back – an unusually modest position for a man who is normally always at the forefront, in good times and bad. He was not talking, but listening; not giving, but receiving instruction and inspiration. The scene looked slightly askew.

After the revelation that no, no one from the government was going to come out and talk to them, they held a ceremonial burning of the *peonada* forms for the cameras, accompanied by a chant of *contra el paro, lucha obrera* (against unemployment, worker's struggle), followed by a rendition of *Andaluces, levantaos*, the Andaluz hymn, sung powerfully and slowly, right fists raised high.

As the crowd mingled and dispersed, and Cañamero did a few interviews, Sánchez Gordillo just seemed to slink off quietly. Some of the SAT trade unionists from outside the *pueblo*, who hadn't met him before, asked to have their photo taken with him. He graciously agreed to each request in turn, shook hands and kissed cheeks, smiling a little wearily, but content to hear their expressions of admiration. He carried the aspect of a jet-lagged celebrity being whisked through a mob of fans to his hotel. And before I could approach him myself, he was gone.

The *Plan de Empleo Rural* (PER), the rural employment plan, is a government social security scheme introduced in the 1980s, designed to subsidise the lack of work in the fields outside of harvest time and prevent another mass exodus from Spain's rural areas. *Jornaleros* who have worked in the field at least thirty-five days, and thus picked up thirty-five *peonadas*, are entitled to six months' social security payment of €400 per month. The olive harvest had been particularly bad that year, however, and it was becoming increasingly difficult for some people to meet that thirty-five-day minimum, and thus, to survive.

The spectre of the early 1980s, and rural families going hungry, was returning with a vengeance. Even the Andalusian PSOE joined SAT and the *marinaleños* in a call on the government to address Andalusian rural poverty and reform the PER, instead of, as Andalusian PSOE number two Mario Jiménez put it, just 'asking the saints and virgins' for salvation.

Eventually, in January 2013, they lowered the qualification for the subsidy to twenty *peonadas* per person. But even that was not enough; and again, it was not just SAT saying so. Spain's biggest union, the CCOO, was also convinced many would not be able to put food on the table. The *peonadas* became the only discussion topic at a number of general assemblies in Marinaleda at the start of 2013. The mayor's CUT colleagues from the local council explained they could fight, and perhaps they should fight – but they must be prepared for the fact that they might not win this one. Calling for across-the-board welfare payments for all poor Andalusian *jornaleros*, irrespective of whether they'd met the twenty days quota, was ideologically and practically necessary; but they could see how bad government finances were – the trend was to make swingeing cuts to social security, not expand it – and the mood in the village was not optimistic.

One thing stood out about these bleak messages about the lack of money coming into the village, something I first noticed at a general assembly in December 2012: the messages weren't being delivered by Sánchez Gordillo. He wasn't in the Sindicato that evening, leading the discussion, as he would have been normally, and he was absent again when the *peonadas* were discussed at further general assemblies in January. I didn't realise it at the time, but Sánchez Gordillo's unusually demure presence, buried in the crowd in Seville that day, was one of his first and last public appearances for months.

Spain is a country that lives to gossip, and the Spanish press and TV had fixated on the Robin Hood mayor all summer – yet they had not yet realised anything untoward was going on with him. It was only when I arrived back in Marinaleda that titbits of information slowly started leaking out of the tightly-bound social networks of the *pueblo*.

The first thing I heard was from someone in Palo Palo, who said when I showed them Sánchez Gordillo's book that they'd heard *el alcalde* was a bit unwell, but were not sure what the problem was. Is that why he didn't seem to be chairing the general assemblies then? I asked León. 'He's not doing them for the moment, no,' León said curtly.

The next day, another *inglesa* arrived in the village, a socialist documentary-maker from London called Uzma. She had asked Gloria, a CUT colleague of Sánchez Gordillo's on the village council, about getting an interview with the mayor, and was told 'he's very stressed at the moment'. The mayor's not really working right now, Gloria explained, and the other councillors are sharing his workload among themselves. 'But what about an interview?' Uzma pressed. She was told to try texting him, and with luck, if he was in the right mood, he might decide to talk to her. He wasn't answering calls or emails. So what about that march to Seville? 'He still does a few small engagements when he feels up to it.'

I put the same questions to Sergio, the youngest Marinaleda councillor, and got the same answers. Sánchez Gordillo was *a little unwell*. He was on indefinite leave – *but I'm sure he'll be back soon*, they kept saying. I came to realise this reassurance was given out of hope, rather than any knowledge about his predicament. I felt sorry for them: they were protecting him, but without really understanding what the problem was. Neither Gloria nor Sergio, nor the staff in the Ayuntamiento and the TV station, knew when the next council meeting would be, or when the next Red Sunday might be, or even when the next (officially weekly) general assembly would be. Meanwhile, they had been arranging the assemblies ad hoc, when necessary, and taking it in turns to officiate. Another councillor, Esperanza, had spoken at one recent village event and at the annual Centro de Adultos dinner, and she handled her new responsibilities very well, people said. It was probably a good thing, one *marinaleño* observed slightly sadly, that the councillors were all getting their first taste of experience in official roles, because *el alcalde* couldn't go on forever. But for now, it was a stretch: the councillors are unpaid, so they all have other jobs, and thus couldn't devote themselves wholeheartedly to taking on mayoral responsibilities.

Life went on, but there were creeping signs of malaise. I took a visiting Belgian photographer for a look around the TV station in the Casa de Cultura, where they used to record Sánchez Gordillo's orations for *Línea Directa*. I asked if we could see inside the studio. They unlocked the doors and flicked on the banks of lights, which crept on as if awaking from a deep sleep; in addition to its 1970s aesthetics, it smelled distinctly musty, like a Cuban-style relic of a fading regime, its glory years left long behind. The studio had not been used in months.

Slowly, more details emerged. As I won the trust of more and more people in the village, and delved behind the polite but firm obfuscations about the mayor's health, I began to collect a variety of theories as to just what on earth had been going on since the August *événements*. Juan Manuel was having family problems, some villagers said, relating either to his ex-wife, his grown-up children, or his new wife and young son – depending on who you talked to. Or he was suffering a deep, placeless depression. Or it was media-induced exhaustion without too much in the way of mental health problems, and he would be back any day now. Sometimes you just have to let a field lie fallow before it yields again, right?

After one of the village's special general assemblies in August 2012, when it was all kicking off, someone casually asked Sánchez Gordillo at the end, 'So, where are you off to now?' Straight after the evening meeting he was driving to Seville, to catch a plane to Madrid for a prime-time TV chat show that night, after that he had to meet some journalists, then he was going to come back on the last flight to Seville and drive back to Marinaleda, so he could get on the coach at 7 am to lead his *pueblo* on the next land occupation. This pattern of relentless direct action, rallies, talks and interviews was repeated every day for about six weeks.

'He's in his sixties now, you know?' one Gordillista said sympathetically, remembering the summer. 'Doing that three-week-long walk, in the summer, is it any wonder he's suffering now? He was doing rallies and interviews and speeches all day, every day. And normally he doesn't just *speak*, calmly – it's like being at the Nuremburg rally.'

She smiled fondly: 'But in a good way, obviously.' During one meeting at the end of September 2012, just before he disappeared from the public stage, and indeed from view, he had reportedly forgotten what he was supposed to be saying, in mid-flow.

'It's depression,' another lifelong *marinaleño* told me confidently. 'But the question is, what is the cause? I think it's because of our economic problems here.' I threw him a confused look: no one had mentioned this as a possibility before – I had come to understand Sánchez Gordillo's problems were entirely personal. 'Sure, there's some of that. But he's worried about the future of the village. There's no money left to pay the employees at El Humoso: they can't pay the *cooperativistas*. I think that's the main problem for the mayor right now.'

The farm is inefficient, he went on, which is why they're losing money; he even went so far as to say El Humoso would work better if a private company ran it. It was heresy for a *marinaleño*. Surely if a private company took over, especially in the midst of the crisis, they'd sack everyone in the drive for efficiency, plant crops like wheat again, and completely defeat the point of the project? 'Well, I think a balance between creating jobs and efficiency in the fields and harvests would be ideal.'

Back in 2011 it had felt as if Marinaleda was separate from the crisis, above the crisis, insulated from its effects by the very thing that had marked them out as different for so many years before. 'No, no, no,' he corrected me. 'If there is less money in Madrid, or in Seville, there is less money here.'

There was some truth to this: as Mariano Rajoy's troika-dictated cuts began to bite, the village's funding from the Junta de Andalucía was drying up fast. The general market downturn, as well as bad luck with recent harvests, was making it ever harder for El Humoso to pay the *jornaleros*, and pay them on time – sometimes they were waiting three months to be paid, and the olive-picking rates were dropping, on top of the problem with the *peonadas*.

Not everyone was quite so pessimistic about the village's prospects, even if they were losing vital government funds. In Palo Palo one evening I got chatting to a young man called Pacheco, Paco to his friends, with a leather jacket, facial hair and a warm sensibility. He was another product of the great 1960s exodus: born in San Sebastian in the Basque country to Andalusian émigrés, they moved back to Marinaleda in the late 1980s when the struggle was taking off. 'I was born in the north, but my heart is *andaluz*,' Paco assured me.

We talked about the crisis in the world outside Marinaleda, and he added his own to the great litany of stories of families, mortgages and businesses in trouble. 'This is an example for the world,' Paco said. 'This right here. Even if things aren't perfect, just look at all the other towns and villages in the crisis. They're suffering because they put profits before people.'

'But Sánchez Gordillo right now – he's not well, is he?'

I asked, slightly tentatively. It's been a very stressful time for him, with all the media attention? 'Yes, but to be fair, he was asking for it,' said Paco. Paco was right – it was never foisted upon the Robin Hood mayor; he chose that path, because of his belief in the struggle, rather than egotistical self-belief. 'He's a . . . peculiar character,' he said eventually, after casting around for the right word. Then he checked himself, wondering if *peculiar* was what he meant. 'He's brave, so brave.'

Before returning to London for Christmas, I wrote to one of the mayor's CUT colleagues, to enquire one last time if I could meet Sánchez Gordillo again. 'Dan,' he wrote back, 'it is impossible now. He is very sick. I hope you can speak with him in January when you come back. I hope you understand, please.' The walls were going up around the *pueblo*. They were fobbing off all requests to see him – whether from the media, documentary-makers, or people wanting to build political bridges from other villages; but his friends and comrades seemed genuinely confident that he just needed a quiet few weeks over the holidays, and he'd be better in the New Year.

Back in London in January, one friend in Marinaleda wrote to me to bring me up to speed. 'Juan Manuel is still keeping quiet and any general assemblies are taken by others and are short and only about work. The financial situation is very bad everywhere and there is no light at the end of the tunnel. Someone told me they think that Juan Manuel is suffering more because he is powerless to alter the position and cannot see a way forward. Even if you can speak to him, I doubt it would be very satisfactory . . . Not much else happening.'

The mood was increasingly sombre. At one general assembly, one of the CUT village councillors, Dolores, had to give the bad news that there would be reduced rates for the annual olive-picking harvest. Some of the *jornaleros* at the meeting thought it would barely cover their travel costs.

When I returned to the village in February 2013, Sánchez Gordillo was still absent. As Antonio made up my room, fitting the sheets with fastidious speed and precision, he asked what I still needed to do on this visit. I mentioned a few things, and that of course, it would be good to speak to *el alcalde* one more time, if possible. He sighed and said, 'Well, good luck. He's still a bit poorly.'

On the second Saturday in February we went to Marinaleda's neighbour *pueblo* El Rubio for their pre-Lenten *carnaval*, on the last Saturday before Lent; it was a very early Easter this year, and thus a very cold *carnaval*. At 7 pm, just after the peach skies turned to blue dusk, the procession began winding through the small town's confusing melee of streets. Just as in Marinaleda, groups of friends wear co-ordinated fancy dress costumes, and there were jellyfish, superheroes, SpongeBob characters, Smurfs, mermaids, cowboys and cross-dressing schoolgirls parading with large measures of rum and coke in hand. The town's parents and grandparents looked on admiringly in warm coats and scarves as the temperature under the cloudless sky abseiled towards zero.

Eventually the parade stopped in El Rubio's Blas Infante park. More drinks were poured, and an eight-piece band of brass and drums competed with a sound system blaring out Spanish dance-pop. As the dusk faded into black and the crowd got progressively merrier, drunken arms were flung around shoulders, and the dancing began – and there, in among the throng, clear as day, was Sánchez Gordillo. After months of absence and confusion, there he was: finally, unmistakably, the Robin Hood mayor, in his red check shirt, keffiyeh, straw hat and tumorous moss of a beard. He had obviously decided to come back to public life in the most befitting way for a man of the people: amid the sociable tumult of the crowd. It was so good to see him out and about again, holding his loud-hailer, leaning on a shopping trolley of supermarket goods – just like in the expropriations the previous summer.

I did a double take. There was Sánchez Gordillo. And there he was again. And again. There were four, no wait, five, no wait, six Sánchez Gordillos. Three of them were having their photo taken with a man in a 'sexy nurse' outfit. One of their beards had fallen off and seemed to be tied to a piece of string. Another one was chatting up one of the mushrooms from the Super Mario Brothers. If this was propaganda of the deed, it was starting to look silly.

I probably shouldn't have been surprised that Sánchez

Gordillo was self-replicating in this way, inspired by Los Gordillos, the Cadiz *chirigota* group. The real people's leader seemed to be absent, but his spirit lived on in ludic fancy dress. At Marinaleda's *carnaval* the following Saturday night, no one was so disrespectful as to reduce their icon – and elected leader – to a caricature. But in his absence he loomed over the *pueblo* and lingered in the air, in half-heard conversations from across the bar, dominating without ever being seen. It seemed to elevate the ominous atmosphere all the more because the locals, many of them friends and comrades of decades' standing, kept referring to him by the honorific title *el alcalde*, not as Juan Manuel.

Midway through a long evening and late night of carnival festivity, we were on our fifth or sixth drink in the Sindicato union bar. I had given in to the repeated insistence from local friends that it didn't matter that I was a) a journalist and b) a foreigner, I had no choice about wearing a costume for carnival. So I was sipping my beer in a monstrous (and unseasonal) Wise Man outfit I'd bought for fifteen euros, trying not to feel self-conscious about being a six-foot-four outsider in a big, flowing, polyester green and turquoise dress, with a homemade silver crown balanced on my head, and a wig of long silvery hair.

The 10 pm *La Liga* kick-off was on the big screen, and local underdogs Granada were somehow beating the mighty Barcelona. *Marinaleños* of all ages mingled happily, tapped their cigarette ash on the floor, and occasionally nodded their heads to the music drifting in from the assembly hall next door, as children hared in and out of the room playing tag.

Just as Barcelona were equalising, someone nudged me gently and leaned in as if imparting a secret. 'Look. It's *el alcalde.*' It was him – actually him this time, talking to a couple on the other side of the bar. He was looking, uncharacteristically, both thin and awkward. Slowly, he circulated the room. Everyone shook his hand and smiled, the older *marinaleños* placed a tender arm on his shoulder – you're looking better, they said – and he smiled and looked a bit shy, a bit overwhelmed, like someone who remembered once having a different relationship with these people, now forgotten. When he reached our part of the room, I greeted him, and we exchanged a few words about my book. He was polite but uncomfortable, like a recently released hostage who had just been let out into the light again and was feeling his way back into social situations.

It had only been a brief outing, and once he'd shown his face, he was gone again. Little changed throughout the spring; he was absent during the *semana cultural* in Easter week, absent from sports and cultural events, and absent from general assemblies and council meetings. The work of the mayor continued to be carried out by his fellow councillors, who waited and hoped for the pall to pass. The bond of trust and solidarity – and ultimately, silence – around the *pueblo* held firm; none of the Spanish right-wing commentators who had been baying for his blood the previous August had even noticed the miniature crisis in Marinaleda. At the very least, Sánchez Gordillo's illness hastened the urgency of questions the village had been ignoring for years: what would happen when their talisman, their leader and comrade, was gone? Could Gordillismo survive without Gordillo, or was he the magic potion that powered the *pueblo*?

The Asterix analogy is actually less glib than it sounds: the village of Marinaleda *is* an implausible, tiny exception to the rule of a seemingly impregnable empire – a liberated space, a labourers' island in a sea of *latifundios*. Unlike Asterix's Gaulish village, however, Marinaleda carries a paradox at its very heart: it is founded on a powerful leadership cult around one truly remarkable individual, but its politics are, above all, the primacy of people power. These politics are sincerely felt, and almost always sincerely executed. Everyone is equal, and everyone fights together, on behalf of everyone; but the *marinaleños* do so most passionately, and most successfully, when Sánchez Gordillo is holding the megaphone.

This is perhaps closer to the continuum of nineteenth-century Andalusian anarchism than it first appears. In the information age, using the mass media in the way Sánchez Gordillo has done is an appropriate and necessary form of 'propaganda of the deed'. The deed itself is integral, whether a hunger strike, an occupation or a raid – but the way it is received is, too. In response to the August supermarket raids, many Spaniards said they thought his methods crude, but far fewer disagreed with his message. Because, for all the mainstream media's flaws, systemic and individual, the question remains: why is it that they fixated on him? Why do Sánchez Gordillo's headline-grabbing actions *work*? In part, perhaps, because he's a charismatic, polarising character; but mostly because people want to hear what he has to say. The megaphone may be shrill, but the words coming out of it have always chimed with the public – all the more so because nobody else in Spanish politics was daring to say them.

Sánchez Gordillo has delivered many fine and memorable epigrams over the years, some of which I have heard in person, in private discussion, or from a platform, and others in speeches or in articles in days of struggle gone by. There are more elegant and profound quotations, but it is this one that sticks with me: 'Because we fight together, because we make our lives together, there is a high degree of good neighbourliness. When we plant trees, we do that together too.' It is this kind of communism that is Marinaleda's triumph – an almost ineffable sense of solidarity.

No one ever forgets 'that strange and moving experience' of believing in a revolution, George Orwell reflected, after arriving in Republican Barcelona on the brink of civil war, a society fizzing with energy as it fleetingly experienced living communism. Marinaleda is neither fully communist nor fully a utopia: but take a step outside the *pueblo* and into contemporary Spain, and you will see a society pummelled, impoverished and atomised, pulled into death and destruction by an economic system and a political class who do not care, and have never cared, whether the poor live or die. Sánchez Gordillo's achievements are more than just the concrete gains of land, housing, sustenance and culture, phenomenal though they are: being there is a strange and moving experience, and, as Orwell suggested, an unforgettable one.

In the eight or so years I have known about Marinaleda, I have sometimes had to remind myself of the gap between the grandiose claims made about the village, by left and right alike, and the humble size and intimacy of the place itself. It is a village which means so much to so many people, across the world; but it has only 2,700 inhabitants, and whole hours can pass where the greatest noise and excitement emanates from a motorcycle speeding down Avenida de la Libertad, or the vocal exercises of a particularly enervated rooster.

It is both poignant and appropriate that Sánchez Gordillo seems to see no bathos, or discrepancy, in devoting as much attention and passion to the local specifics of the *pueblo* – the need to start planting artichokes this month, not pimentos – as he does to the big picture, persuading the world that only an end to capitalism will restore dignity to the lives of billions.

The big hitters of the Spanish mainstream press might not have noticed that Sánchez Gordillo was unwell, but the steady stream of left-wing enthusiasts visiting the village were finding out upon arrival. At a table outside Bar Gervasio I watched Sergio, the smart young councillor with the black stubble and the black jeans, unblinkingly try to explain to Uzma, the British documentary-maker, that it was 'normal in political life to be away sometimes'. I don't know where he is, and he's ill, Sergio explained; 'I'm not connected with him.'

'*Hombre*, you're famous!' shouted one of Sergio's young friends as he walked past us. Sergio looked sort of proud and embarrassed at the same time. In his mid-twenties, he's by far the youngest councillor in the village, though only a decade younger than the new leader of IU, Alberto Garzón – a man identified more with the *indignados* than with established party politics. The future political direction of this generation, who not only do not remember fascism, but were not yet born when Franco died, is going to be critical to Spain's future – not least because they are the ones weathering the jaw-dropping 57 per cent rate of youth unemployment and awkwardly squeezing back into corners of their parents' homes.

Sergio recalled his mother telling him they were on strike when he was three years old. He did not, he laughed, know what it meant, but remembered noticing even then that something in the routine of his young life was different. 'By the time I was twelve or thirteen, I was conscious about the situation in the village, and how it was different from other villages, from talking to my sister and my mother, and going on my first demonstrations. I remember so many demonstrations, so many. The big one was when I was eighteen, going to Seville, and being in the big city, in front of the parliament of Andalusia. Seeing power for the first time was a revelation. I realised politics must be more than just passively choosing between two identical parties.'

His scepticism about all mainstream politics is that of an ever-growing majority in Spain. 'A pox on all their houses' has become more than just an offhand expression of apathy, so common in Western capitalist countries: it is an increasingly fervently held wish, as contempt is transformed into anger. For Sergio, the most important issue facing Marinaleda during the crisis was, in a sense, the same as it ever was: trying to persuade the central authority that work, shelter, culture, and life without undue interference – whether you call that freedom or autonomy – were all basic human rights.

'Marinaleda has been important twice in its hundreds of years of history. The first time was in the late 1970s and early 1980s, when we had the Transition, and that was a crisis really, a crisis of democracy, trying to find a way out of the fascist state, a way out of dictatorship. Right now, this is Marinaleda's second moment. Look at the rest of Spain. During the better economic times, people weren't watching us. Now they are all coming here. It's an economic crisis, a political crisis, a crisis of corruption – it's a systemic crisis.'

'Are you optimistic about the village?' I asked, alluding to the situation with the *peonadas*, and the collapse in funding they were getting from Seville.

'The situation with work is critical right now,' he agreed. 'It's complicated, with the *peonadas*, but critical. But of course I'm optimistic. If I wasn't, I wouldn't be working on this project. It's a real alternative to the crisis, and I believe the rest of the capitalist world can be different, too. I'm aware that Marinaleda has advantages and disadvantages, but we can be an example.'

He cited their achievements again, with the same matter-of-fact confidence that Sánchez Gordillo always displays when talking about seizing the land, building houses, and reclaiming culture for the people. Are your fellow villagers optimistic too? I asked.

'Yes, of course. They know the situation is critical. In the past Marinaleda received a lot of benefits from Seville to help create jobs, and now they are being taken away, because of the crisis of capitalism. But the *pueblo*, they know we fought – we all fought – for our needs and rights before, and it's necessary to do so again.'

It's not quite back to square one, back to 1980, but I was starting to see Sergio's rationale. This was Marinaleda's second great crisis-opportunity. You have a big burden, I said, you're making a big promise, if you think you can sustain the utopia in this context. He laughed – at me, this time.

'Are you serious? We've been fighting for thirty years, and we promised all this, back then. Look at what the village was like thirty years ago, and look what it has become through struggle.'

He stopped short of saying, 'Ha, your feeble crisis of capitalism is nothing,' but I got the feeling he wanted to. The odds stacked against them in 1975, when Franco died, were certainly far, far greater, and this brazen revolution-ary confidence is going to be essential to the village's future.

We ordered another round of drinks, and Uzma pestered Sergio some more about when she might be able to meet Sánchez Gordillo; he buffered and stalled, perhaps a little weary of his role as gatekeeper, espe-cially since his instructions were clearly to keep the gate firmly shut. I tried to swerve the conversation away from the mayor.

For my book, Sánchez Gordillo is not everything, I said to him. I'm more interested in the people, the *pueblo*, as a collec-tive, and what they have achieved – not just the one man.

'Okay,' he said, gravely, 'but you've got to understand who we're talking about here. Quite simply, everything Marinaleda has won is thanks to Sánchez Gordillo. That is evident. Everything we have made, it's thanks to him.'

It felt almost like I was getting told off for having the temerity to shift the credit for their victories from the leader to his followers – for daring to underestimate his influence. 'But one day,' I started, 'well, the day will have to come when he . . .' Sergio cut me off.

'When he's no longer leader, in the future, the project

will continue. The project is still the same, to create a utopia, and that will continue.'

He stopped.

'But the day has not come yet.'

Acknowledgements

Thanks to my parents, Helen and Rod, for advice and support beyond the call of duty, to my sister Sally across the other side of the world and to my wonderful friends for putting up with me while I was writing this.

Thanks to Dave Stelfox for photographs and solidarity in the form of hot cheese; to Steve Bloomfield, Tan Copsey, Paul Fleckney, Cat O'Shea and all previous and honorary members of the Republic of Florence for their patience and good humour (you're an acknowledgement); to Daniel Trilling for his ever-wise counsel; to Anthony Barnett, Alice Bell, Melissa Bradshaw, Heleina Burton, Joe Caluori, Ally Carnwath, Adrian Cornell du Houx, Valeria Costa-Kostritsky, Anna Fielding, Sam Geall, Rosa Gilbert, Paul Gilroy, Alex Hoban, Tom Humberstone, Jamie Mackay, Alex Macpherson, Phil Oltermann, Jen Paton, Laurie Penny, Kirsty Simmonds, Alex Sushon, Kanishk Tharoor, Vron Ware, Bella Waugh, Nick Wilson and Chris Wood for listening to me witter on; to my editor Leo Hollis at Verso, as well as Federico Campagna, Huw Lemmey, Mark

Martin, Lorna Scott Fox, Sarah Shin, Rowan Wilson, and my agent Sophie Lambert at Conville and Walsh. Shouts also to the people keeping my brain switched on in London, in particular everyone at openDemocracy, the Deterritorial Support Group and Novara Media.

I'm forever grateful to everyone who talked to me across Spain in the last few years – and especially to all the people who bought me beer, took me on marches, gave me lifts, talked politics with me, and made me lentils and chorizo. Thanks in particular to Marcel and Karine at Can Serrat in El Bruc, Ian Mackinnon in Madrid, Carlos Delclós, the Artefakte gang, Jaime Casas and Tom Clarke in Barcelona, Juanjo Alcalde, Emma Herrera Ortiz and Paulette Soltani in Sevilla, Javi Rivero and his family in Estepa, and Chris and Ali Burke, Antonio Porquera Tejada and Cristina Martín Saavedra in the village.

Thanks above all to the people of Marinaleda.